Stone Crosses

in

North Cor

by

Andrew Langdon

DYFFRESYAS CROWSOW

PROTECTOR OF CROSSES

First published in 1992 by The Federation of Old Cornwall Societies

This Second Edition published in 1996 by Andrew Langdon

ISBN No. 0 9528684 0 7

Typeset by the Author

Printed by Quill Graphics, Padstow

This book is dedicated to my daughters, Emma and Nicola

Acknowledgements

It would not be possible to complete this work without the help and support of many friends. I am indebted to Mrs Gillian Clark for proof reading my manuscript.

To Miss Angela Broome, Librarian at the Royal Institution of Cornwall's Courtney Library for her help and assistance and Mr Collin Brewer of Egloshayle for the loans of material from his personal library collection.

To members of various Old Cornwall Societies who have gone to great lengths to encourage this work, in particular to Mr Rob Evans the Federation of Old Cornwall Societies Publications Officer and Mr John Neale of Launceston OCS for their continuing help in promoting and distributing my work.

To my wife Elaine for having to put up with my endless visits to ancient monuments, where ever we go on holiday and for her help in typing and distributing my work.

For photographs I acknowledge my brother Adrian Langdon, Miss Ruth Hirst, the late Mr Frank Smeeth, the late Miss Mary Henderson and the late Mr Ken Baker.

To Mr. Brian Bawden for help, advice and company while visiting many of Cornwall's stone crosses, and to Messrs D. Attwell, T. Dingle and C. David the staff of North Cornwall Heritage Coast & Countryside Service for their help and encouragement.

To the executive committee of the Federation of Old Cornwall Societies for promoting the original edition of this work and for supporting the additional volumes in this series.

To the many landowners who have kindly given me access and made me welcome to view their crosses and the numerous members of the public who have helped me in my quest to seek out further lost crosses

To the many friends who have helped with the restoration of North Cornwall's crosses during the last decade, in particular to Mr David Attwell NCHCCS, Ms Ann Preston-Jones CAU, Mr Noel Hill, Mr Ray Burrows, Mr & Mrs Lawrence & Sue Kelland, Mr Harold Barriball and the late Mr George Cowling and the late Mr Frank Smeeth.

To Lady Molesworth - St. Aubyn of Pencarrow Estate for allowing me to use a photograph of the Pencarrow Cross on the front cover.

Finally, and the most important, to the anonymous benefactor who has most generously agreed to loan me financial support to publish this 2nd edition.

ANDREW LANGDON
Egloshayle
Wadebridge

Contents

Preface

The author has written this short guide on stone crosses in the hope of encouraging readers to take a more active role in preserving part of Cornwall's unique heritage. In recent years several stone crosses have been stolen or sold to unscrupulous dealers, robbing the county of its irreplaceable past. The demand for granite monuments and artefacts has grown into a lucrative market and reports of the theft of granite millstones, troughs and staddle stones (mushrooms) are on the increase throughout the county. The author believes that the only way to curtail this rape of the county's antiquities is by encouraging residents and visitors alike to take an interest in these stones. If the monuments are visited more regularly by members of the public, their protection may well be improved.

This book is set out as a Gazetteer giving details of public access, its situation, and a brief description and history of each cross. It is not the author's aim to produce a definitive work, but just an up-to-date guide for visitors to the stones. The guide includes general information on the Cornish crosses, such as the different types of cross, reasons for erecting the monuments, probable age etc. The gazetteer is arranged in alphabetical order of parishes, and each cross is recorded under its ecclesiastical parish and not by its civil parish. This is to reduce any confusion with previous studies which have all been based on the ecclesiastic or church parish rather than the administrative parish.

The guide loosely covers the North Cornwall area (see attached map), although some parishes have been omitted and the author hopes to include these in a future guide. All sites are recorded with their National (eight figure) Grid Reference to enable visitors to use any scale of Ordnance Survey map.

For the purpose of making comparisons or identifying previously recorded crosses, the author has noted all measurements of the crosses in imperial, together with an approximate metric conversion. The height of a cross may vary considerably over a period of time, if soil is removed or built up, but other dimensions will remain constant unless the stone is damaged. In the case of measuring the head of a Latin cross, the measurement is taken across the horizontal limbs. All monuments can be assumed to be cut from moorland granite unless otherwise stated.

Since the publication of the first edition of this work, one new cross has been discovered at St.Clether and is numbered 24A, therefore maintaining the same sequence of numbering for both editions.

Maps

There are three 1:50 000 Ordnance Survey maps required to cover the area included in this guide book, or nine 1:25 000 maps. There is also an Explorer O/S Map of Bodmin Moor.

Explorer Series	Sheet No.	9	Bodmin Moor	
Landranger Series	Sheet No.	190	Bude and Clovelly	
		200	Newquay and Bodmin	
		201	Plymouth and Launceston	
Pathfinder Series	Sheet No.	1273	(SS21/31)	Kilkhampton
		1292	(SS20/30)	Bude and Holesworthy
		1310	(SX19)	St. Gennys
		1325	(SX08/18)	Camelford
		1326	(SX28/38)	Launceston
		1337	(SW87/97)	Padstow and Wadebridge
		1338	(SX07/17)	Bodmin Moor West
		1346	(SW86/96)	Newquay
		1347	(SX06/16)	Bodmin

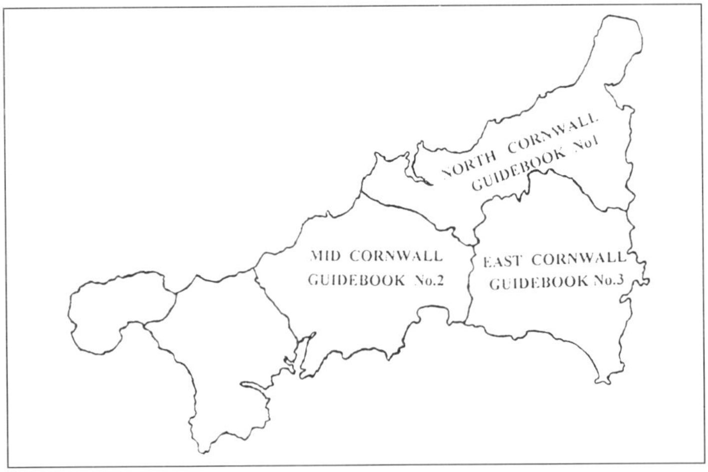

Area covered by the North Cornwall Guide

THE ANCIENT ECCLESIASTICAL PARISHES OF NORTH CORNWALL COVERED IN THIS GUIDE

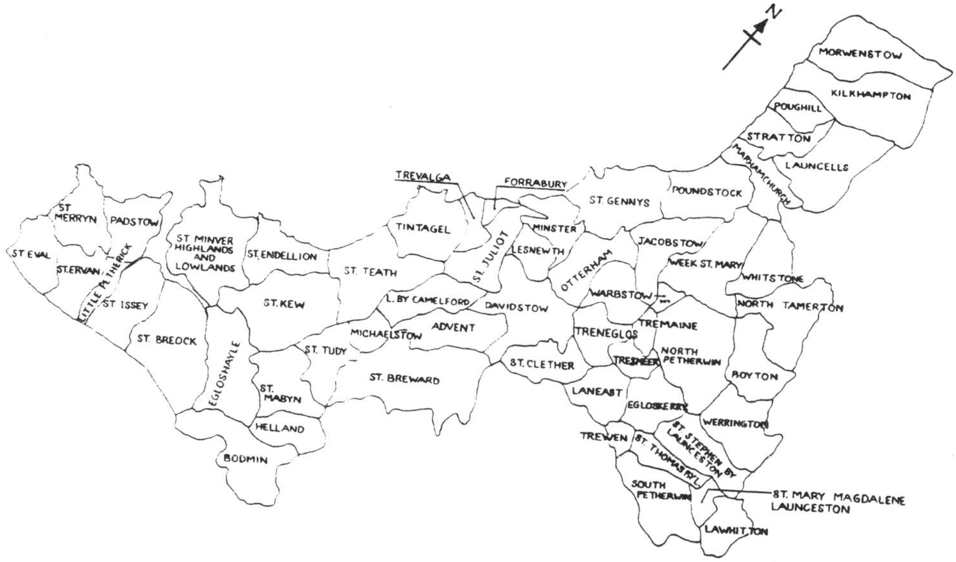

Introduction

There has been a great deal written about Cornwall's ancient stone crosses over the last century, although most works are either out of print or unpublished manuscripts. This has prompted the author to produce this up to date guide book to aid both visitor and residents alike who are interested in these early Christian monuments.

In 1856 John T. Blight of Penzance published a book called, *"The Ancient Crosses and Antiquities of West Cornwall"*, and two years later followed this with a second volume on East Cornwall. In 1872 a second edition combined both volumes under one cover. Many of the North Cornwall crosses were also illustrated by Sir John Maclean in his three volume work on the parochial and family history of the *"Deanery of Trigg Minor"*, published in 1873, 1876 and 1879 respectively. Trigg Minor consisted of twenty North Cornwall parishes in 1873 and Maclean gave descriptions and illustrations of all the known early Christian monuments and crosses in that area. He also gave an account of the ancient tracks and roads which many of the crosses once marked.

The most impressive and complete work on Cornish crosses was by Arthur G. Langdon in 1896, entitled *"Old Cornish Crosses"*. In his book Langdon recorded 360 monuments with scaled illustrations of 286 of them, giving a detailed account of their history, style and decoration. He also noted many other Gothic crosses and base stones and was recognised as the leading authority on the subject of Cornish crosses at the beginning of the century. In 1988 a facsimile of *"Old Cornish Crosses"* was reprinted and although still a most important reference book, at least 130 of the crosses recorded have been either shifted, damaged, renovated or lost since 1896. Langdon also published many additional papers on the subject of crosses, including a chapter in the *Victoria County History of Cornwall* on early Christian monuments, recording crosses discovered since his original work.

During his short life Charles Henderson (1900 - 1933), perhaps the most well-known Cornish historian, continued to discover new crosses. He wrote a great deal of additional notes on the subject of crosses, including a supplement to Langdon's work. Later in 1938 a book was published entitled *"Cornish Crosses, Christian and Pagan"*, in which, using Langdon's illustrations, T.F.G. Dexter gave a pagan interpretation to many of the monuments. By the 1950s there were many more historians researching the Cornish crosses. Between 1952 and 1968, Surgeon Captain G.E. Ellis published his work on the East Cornwall crosses in the bi-annual journal, *"Devon and Cornwall Notes & Queries"*. In 1961 Major R.D. Baird and Lady White completed their work on the Cornish crosses, which in manuscript form was presented to the Royal Institution of Cornwall's Courtney Library. In 1973 Laura Rowe wrote the only guide book on crosses, covering the stones in the West Cornwall area.

The most complete work was compiled by Mary Henderson in 1983, who spent an astonishing 30 years on the project. Miss Henderson catalogued over 600 ancient stones, tracing their history through ancient documents and manuscripts. Unfortunately Miss Henderson's four volume work has not been published but is available to the serious student at the Royal Institution of Cornwall, along with a volume of fine pen and ink illustrations by Laura Rowe.

The author would like to point out that it is only a coincidence that he bears the same name (A.G. Langdon) as that of the Victorian historian and author of *"Old Cornish Crosses"*. Similarly, there is no family connection between Charles Henderson and Mary Henderson. For a complete list of further reading on Cornwall's stone crosses please see Bibliography.

1i Reasons for Erecting Stone Crosses

Cornwall is a unique county with its own language and culture, and is rich in legends and mysteries. An abundance of ancient monuments and antiquities can be found throughout the Duchy, especially in the more barren and exposed areas such as the Penwith peninsula and Bodmin Moor. One of the most prolific of Cornwall's ancient monuments is the stone cross which cannot be seen anywhere else in the country in such numbers or variety. There are over four hundred complete stone crosses standing in the county and at least two hundred heads, shafts and base stones.

a) WAYSIDE CROSSES - The most common type of Cornish cross is the wayside cross, which as its name implies stands on the side of roads, ancient tracks and footpaths. Its main function was to mark the route to the parish church. Wherever one lived in medieval Cornwall, unless wealthy enough to own a horse, one had in most cases to walk to church. Many farms and hamlets had their "short cuts" to the churchtown and these later became public rights of way. This is why many of Cornwall's public footpaths went from farm to farm, taking the most direct route to the church. The wayside cross was also used to mark tracks to sites of pilgrimage, to monasteries, priories, ancient chapels and holy wells. By the 19th century the county was criss-crossed by hundreds of footpaths and tracks forming an elaborate network, which in some cases linked many parishes. It is still possible to walk for many miles in Cornwall on footpaths, without touching a metalled road.

The footpaths were not only used on Sundays for attending church, but as a general right of way. Several of the mother churches were remote from the centres of population, and in such cases a coffin would be carried miles along church paths to the church for burial. An example of this is St. Ives which, until the early 15th century, had to bury all its parishioners at the mother church in Lelant, three miles from the fishing port. The chapel did not gain full parochial status until 1576, i.e. it did not obtain the rights to perform baptisms and burials until that time. Therefore, the church paths between St. Ives and Lelant were frequently used by funeral processions. Some of these footpaths in the county are still known as Coffin Paths. When the funeral cortege walked the church paths to the parish church, it was usual to stop at each cross so that prayers could be said and so that the bearers could take a rest. Wealthy merchants when passing a cross would sometimes leave alms for the poor. A cross in St. Agnes churchyard, according to Blight, was used as a lych stone to rest the coffin on, prior to entering the church. Again, the church at St. Agnes did not obtain the right of burial until 1482, and therefore all the inhabitants of the village had to be taken to Perranzabuloe for burial.

In addition, the wayside cross was also used to mark the main tracks or highways of the day. Many tracks connected priories together or marked tracks to monasteries and other ecclesiastical establishments. One such monastery was that of St. Michael on St. Michael's Mount near Marazion, where a Benedictine monastery was established by 1135 and the site had been a special place of pilgrimage from the Dark Ages. On the sands of Marazion there is a rock known as Chapel Rock which, it is said, pilgrims used as the last shrine before visiting the Mount.

Half way across the Causeway, between Chapel Rock and the Mount, is the base of an ancient cross, still in situ beside the Causeway. It is said that the cross was broken down in a storm in 1750.

The wayside cross was sometimes used to mark other ancient sites such as holy wells, chapels and baptisteries. A Latin cross still stands next to the holy well at St. Cleer on Bodmin Moor, and another cross stands near a footpath to Madron Well near Boswarthen Farm in Madron parish. Crosses are also sometimes placed beside the banks of rivers to mark a safe fording place. At St. Clether on the east side of Bodmin Moor, a footpath crosses the River Inney and a large round headed cross stands on the south bank marking shallow water and a firm footing.

b) BOUNDARY CROSSES - Another reason for the large number of crosses around the Cornish countryside is due to the fact that the stones were also used to mark boundaries. Crosses were set up to mark parish boundaries and the boundaries of the Glebe land. It is also possible that they may have marked monastic land and even church sanctuaries. Callywith cross at Bodmin still marks the parish boundary between Bodmin and Cardinham On Tregonetha Downs a cross known as "Cross and Hand" stands at the intersection of three parish boundaries; that of St. Columb Major, St. Wenn and Roche. At Cardinham the glebe land is also marked by crosses, four in total, and Rostigan cross is mentioned as a bound stone of glebe land at St. Wenn. In West Penwith, St. Buryan was one of four parishes in Cornwall which had a sanctuary extending beyond the walls of the church. It has been suggested by Croft Andrew that a double ring of crosses marked the extent of the sanctuary limits. This may be why St. Buryan boasts more ancient crosses than any other parish in Cornwall

c) MEMORIAL CROSSES - There are a number of inscribed stones and inscribed crosses in the county, most of which were erected as a memorial to some local king or chieftain. One of the most famous memorial crosses in the Duchy is the King Doniert Stone at St. Cleer, which is the pedestal of a fine 9th century Celtic cross. An earlier inscribed cross at St. Endellion was erected in memory of Brocagni, and another at Lanteglos by Camelford dedicated to someone called Aelwine.

d) CHURCHYARD CROSSES - The most elaborate crosses in the Duchy are usually found in our parish churchyards. In many cases the churchyard or burial ground existed before the building of a church or oratory and was known as a 'lan'. A lan is a raised cemetery or burial ground, usually oval in shape and of great antiquity, as the raised level indicates many centuries of burials. Many parishes still take their names from this prefix followed by the name of the Saint to whom the church was dedicated e.g. Lanhydrock (Lan-Hydroc), Lanivet (Lan-Nevet). The prefix Llan in Wales suggests the same meaning.

These crosses may have been erected to mark the Christian burial site, prior to the building of the church. Today most of them pre-date the existing fabric of their churches. The crosses were also set up in the churchyard as preaching crosses for the early Christians to congregate around to hear the readings of the Gospel. The majority of the crosses were large monuments and were usually decorated rather than plainly carved like the wayside and boundary crosses. The setting up of churchyard crosses continued through the centuries, and as late as the 15th century lantern crosses were being erected in the churchyards, e.g. St. Mawgan in Pyder, and St. Mary Magdalene in Launceston.

e) VILLAGE/MARKET CROSSES - In Cornwall there are only a few true village or market crosses, although in some cases a wayside cross has been adapted for this function. They were usually set up by the religious authorities as a reminder of Our Lord during their day to day secular life. There is the remains of a village cross at St. Ewe, on a stepped base, which is still one of the focal points of the village. In the past, proclamations would be read at the village cross and public meetings conducted there. At many of these crosses merchants sold their goods and therefore we acquire the name Market Cross. In some English counties these are called Butter Crosses, due to the fact that butter and eggs were sold there e.g. Winchester; at Salisbury the cross is known as the Poultry Cross. Taxes and market dues were paid at the cross and the collectors, representing either the Lord of the Manor or a religious house, occasionally had elaborate shelters built over the cross to protect themselves from the weather.

Gothic style structures and canopies can still be seen in many English villages, made of timber or stone, and even if a conventional cross did not exist, the structures were still known as Market Crosses, e.g. Dunster in Somerset, Malmesbury in Wiltshire, and Newport. St Stephen by Launceston is the only example of a market cross enclosed by a canopy in Cornwall.

ii The Different Styles of Cornish Crosses

There are many varieties and styles of Cornish cross, and each can be catalogued by its shape and decoration into one or more main groups. These main groups can also be sub-divided into smaller groups depending on decoration. Some of the unornamented crosses fit into one main group only, but others can be classified under many groups. The most important point to realise is that every cross is unique and that crosses in the same parish or locality may be similar but none are exactly the same.

a) INSCRIBED CROSSES - There are approximately 60 early Christian inscribed stones in the county, of which twenty are inscribed crosses. The majority of the inscribed crosses display some type of Latin script, with the exception of the Castle Goff stone at Lanteglos by Camelford which bears a Saxon inscription. One interesting example is the Longcross at St. Endellion, which displays a Chi Rho monogram (see Dating of Crosses) and a bi-lingual inscription in Latin and Ogham. Ogham (Ogam) is an ancient Irish alphabet of twenty characters formed by parallel strokes either side of or across a continuous line. In the case of standing stones and crosses, the continuous line is usually the vertical edge of the shaft. (Fig. 1).

b) CROSS SLABS AND PILLARS - There are a few stones in Cornwall which, although they display a cross on them, do not conform to any of the popular shapes identified with Cornish crosses. The Tregurnow stone at St. Buryan and a similar wedge-shaped stone at Lower Drift, Sancreed are large slabs of granite with crosses cut on them. A rectangular slab of granite at St. Columb Major churchyard has four triangular incisions cut on it to form a cross. At St. Columb Minor a stone shaped like a pillar exists which is almost round in section but displays a cross on each side. Another at Forrabury has a cross cut on only one face.

c) LATIN CROSSES - These existed right through the Cornish stone cross period, the most rudimentary of these are Lambrenny at Davidstow, Godolphin at the Church and Boscathnoe at Madron. All three stones are roughly hewn with short stubby limbs and in the case of Godolphin a small incised Latin cross is displayed on its head. Later the Latin crosses became more uniform in shape; a well proportioned stone is Treglines cross in the churchyard at St. Minver. Even at the end of the medieval era Latin crosses were still being erected, although by this time they were octagonal in section. The semi-Gothic Latin cross is found more frequently in the south-eastern side of the county, from Grampound area to St. Germans and Saltash.

d) ROUND OR WHEEL HEADED CROSSES - This group can be sub-divided into many different types, depending mainly on the way the cross is formed on the head. Sometimes a crucifix is displayed; in other cases equal limbed or Latin crosses are cut, either in relief or incised. These form the majority of the wayside and boundary crosses. Fig. 2. shows examples of some of the different types to be seen.

e) HOLED CROSSES - There are again many different examples; at Phillack the churchyard cross displays a four holed cross head, but only the upper two holes are pierced right through.

At. Egloshayle there is a cross known as the Three Hole Cross; this monument displays four holes cut in the vertical and horizontal positions to form a diagonal of St. Andrew's Cross, but the lower hole is not completed. A similar cross, known as St. Piran's Cross at Perranzabuloe, again has not had the lower hole completed. The more elaborate churchyard crosses have their holes formed by an outer ring enclosing the limbs of the cross. These range from the delicately executed Michaelstow Churchyard cross, to the massive and solid looking cross head at St. Michael's, Porthilly.

f) LANTERN CROSSES - There are only five complete lantern crosses in the County, although there are cross heads and fragments of at least another ten. The earliest appears to be the Churchtown cross at St. Erth, which is a transition between the ancient wayside crosses and the lantern type. The monument is made of granite but is only worked on two faces. Granite lantern crosses also exist at St. Ives, Callington and Lanteglos by Fowey. The highly developed lantern crosses at St. Neot and St. Mawgan in Pydar are cut from Cataclewse greenstone from the Cataclewse quarry near St. Merryn, which allows fine carving to be achieved. The decoration on the lantern crosses all follow a similar format with the predominate face displaying the Crucifixion scene. The reverse face usually depicts the Virgin Mary and Child, while the remaining faces show single figures.

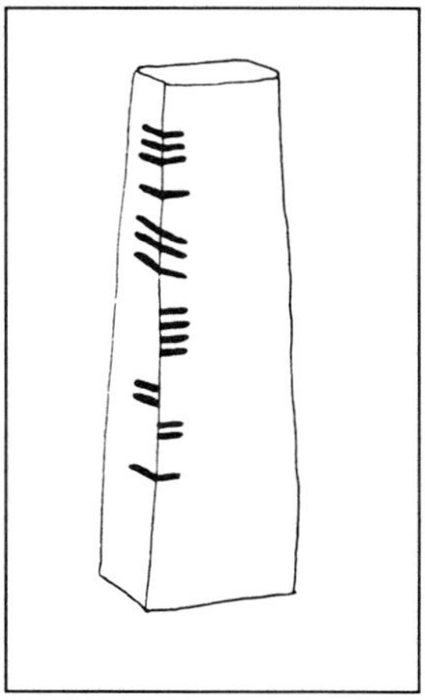

Fig. 1 Ogham Inscription

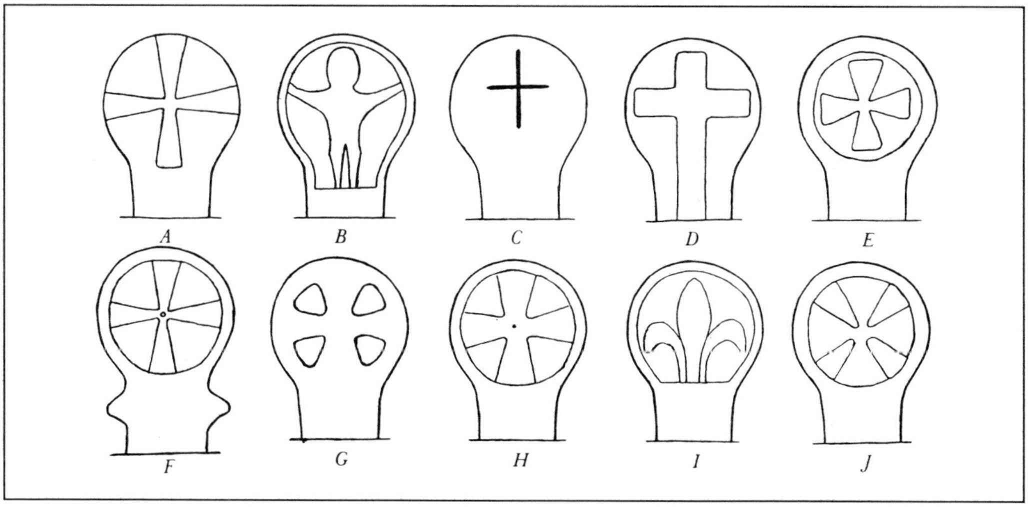

Fig. 2. This illustration shows a few of the many styles of wheel headed cross in Cornwall.

A.- Cross Hill, St. Mabyn , B.- .Rosemorran, Gulval, C.- Trenuggo Hill, Sancreed, D.- Mabe Churchyard, E.- Menabilly, Tywardreath , F.- Cross Gates, St. Clether, G.- Lower Woodley, Lanivet, H.- Castle Hill Street, Bodmin., I..- Washaway, Egloshayle, J.- Egloshayle Churchyard

iii Probable age of Crosses

It is extremely difficult to determine the exact age of these stone crosses, and even the professional historians and archaeologists sometimes differ in their opinion. The only clues we have to help us to date the stones are:

1. if they are named in an ancient document which is dated,
2. if the monument displays an inscription that can be dated, or
3. by the style and type of decoration.

One of the earliest Christian symbols is the Chi Rho monogram, which consists of the first two letters of the name Christ written in Greek. The monogram featured on many Roman coins and mosaics, as well as European pottery during the 4th and 5th centuries. It has been suggested by historians that after the monogram died out in Gaul (central Europe) it may have continued to be illustrated on stones in Britain until the early 6th century (Fig. 3).

Cornwall has four early Christian stones displaying the Chi Rho; a fifth found at St. Helen's Oratory, St. Just in Penwith, has since been lost. A stylised version of the monogram is displayed at Phillack. It is therefore possible to predict a probable date for these stones.

One Cornish cross which can be dated with some accuracy as pre-Norman is the St. Piran's cross on Penhale Sands, Perranzabuloe. This large cross was mentioned in a Charter dated 960 AD in the reign of King Edgar, and called Cristel Mael. It was then recorded as a bound stone for the parish of Tywarnhale, which was an ancient parish stretching from St. Agnes to Illogan, including Perranzabuloe.

The King Doniert stone at St. Cleer is an inscribed cross pedestal set up as a memorial to Doniert who died in AD 875, and therefore can be dated as 9th century.

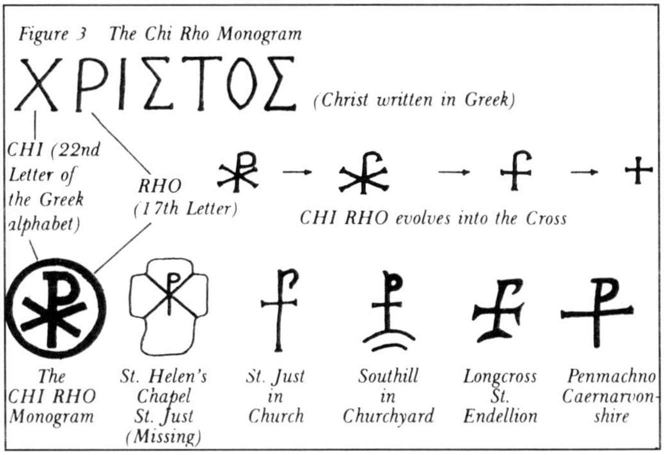

Fig. 3 The Chi Rho Monogram

The decoration on crosses can also play a large part in dating them when compared with examples of known date in other Celtic areas. Decoration such as plaitwork, interlace and key patterns on crosses can also be seen in other Celtic artwork and ancient monastic manuscripts, giving some guide to dating although many medieval crosses have been copied from earlier examples making dating more difficult.

The majority of Cornwall's crosses are said to date from between the 9th and 13th centuries, although some of the inscribed crosses and slabs may be earlier. We know from documentary evidence that wayside crosses were still being erected as late as the middle 15th century. Dr. Reginald Mertherdewa, who was Principal of Bull Hall in Oxford and Rector of Creed parish, bequeathed money for the erection of new wayside crosses. His will, dated 14th February 1447, read:

"..... new stone crosses are to be put up, of the usual kind, in those parts of Cornwall from Kayar Berlasek to Camborne church, where dead bodies are rested on their way to burial, that prayers maybe made, and the bearers take some rest."

It must be appreciated that there was no clear cut end to one style and the beginning of another. The changes in style and decoration were slowly phased in over many centuries and not all at once, making it even more difficult to assume their date.

iv Distribution of Monuments

Almost ninety per cent of stone crosses in Cornwall are cut from surface moorland granite, and therefore it is not surprising that the majority of the stones are to be found near the moorland areas of the county. The West Penwith Moor and Bodmin Moor is where we find the largest concentration of stone crosses, although there are also smaller concentrations of stones around the Wendron Moor and Blackmoor areas. (Fig. 4 and Fig. 5). Another reason for the large number of crosses in these areas may be due to the sites of important early religious houses.

The eastern side of Cornwall, including the parishes bordering the river Tamar, are sparsely endowed with crosses. The south-eastern area, i.e. from Veryan to Sheviock, displays much later examples of monuments, most considered to be semi-Gothic in date. Wheel headed wayside and boundary crosses depicting figures or the Crucifixion scene, are found exclusively in West Cornwall, any found to the east of Truro (e.g. Lanherne, St. Mawgan in Pydar), have usually been re-sited from the west.

The early missionaries from Wales and Ireland who visited Cornwall in the Dark Ages, founded many small settlements and cells on the north coast of our county. This may be why we have many crosses and early Christian monuments around the Hayle and the Camel - the two main rivers on the north coast.

Obviously it was possibly to move crosses from one area to another, but in the majority of cases a cross would be cut from available surface stone as close as possible to where the monument was to be sited. In a few cases other material such as Pentewan stone, greenstone, sandstone and even slate stone have been used to carve Cornish crosses.

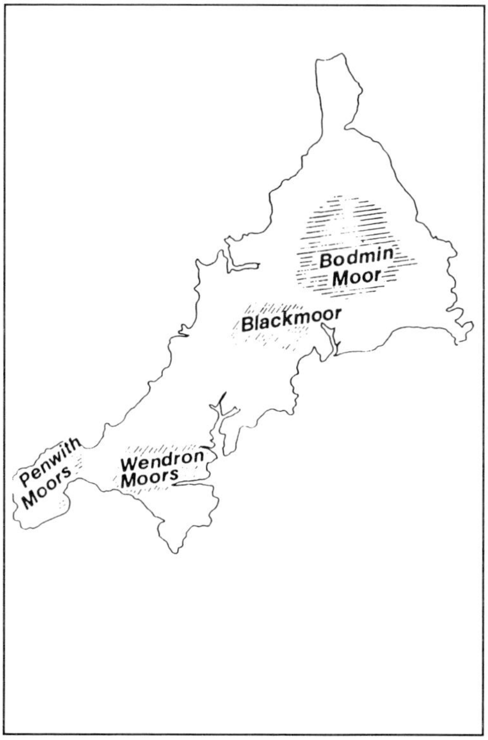

Fig. 4 Moorland areas of Cornwall

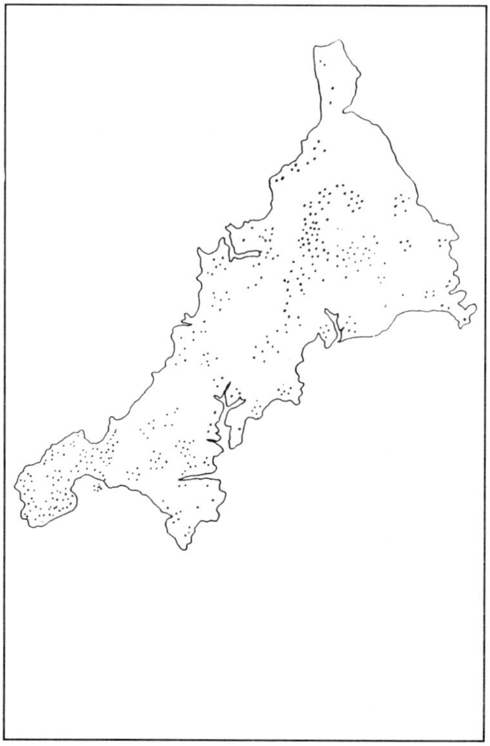

Fig. 5 Distribution of Crosses in Cornwall

2i Preservation by Old Cornwall Societies

The first Old Cornwall Society was founded at St. Ives in 1920, its aim being to record and preserve all things Cornish such as dialect words, traditions, folk lore and its ancient monuments. The Society organised winter lectures and summer pilgrimages and this practice has continued through to this day. The Society was an immediate success and the formation of additional societies rapidly followed, with Truro and Redruth in 1922 and Hayle, Camborne and St. Just in 1923. In 1924 there were eight societies and this led to the forming of the Federation of Old Cornwall Societies, which today boasts 47 societies. It's motto in Cornish is:

"CUNTELLEUGH AN BREWYON US GESYS NA VO KELLYS TRAVYTH"
which translated reads:

"GATHER YE THE FRAGMENTS THAT ARE LEFT, THAT NOTHING BE LOST."

In April 1925 the Federation published its first journal and has continued ever since, producing them half yearly in Spring and Autumn. Many reports on the discovery of stone crosses have featured in these journals along with all aspects of local history. Today there are also Cornish Associations in other parts of Britain, affiliated to the Federation, and as far away as South Australia.

In North Cornwall there are six societies and they have renovated, re-erected and preserved many crosses through the enthusiasm of their members. In 1932, one of North Cornwall's oldest Christian monuments was rescued by the Bodmin O.C.S. from its unsuitable site at Doyden Head, and brought back to its original site at Longcross, St. Endellion. In 1938 the founder society, St. Ives, gave financial aid to a project to re-erect a cross in the parish of Warbstow.

Wadebridge O.C.S. was formed in 1932 and for many years took responsibility for the ancient monuments of 19 parishes in North Cornwall. Their first project was to re-erect the Three Hole Cross at Egloshayle, when road alterations necessitated its removal and repositioning in 1939. Later in 1947, Wadebridge formed a cross sub-committee to help negotiate and organise the renovation and erection of three crosses, Trequite and Job's Cross at St. Kew and Penwine Cross in St. Mabyn parish.

One of the society's most enthusiastic members was their President, Mr. Nicholas Bray of St. Kew, who was responsible for the discovery of Job's Cross in 1906, and its subsequent rescue. He also was instrumental in the erection of the Polrode Cross in St. Kew churchyard in 1908 and later the discovery of the lower section of this monument in 1926. In 1939 Mr. Bray was influential in the renovation of the Three Hole Cross and was also involved with the examination of the Tresloggett Cross at St. Mabyn. Mr. Bray was present at the re-dedication of Trequite Cross, which together with members of the Cross Committee, helped to erect in 1947. He was also involved in the preliminary stages of re-erecting Job's Cross, prior to his death in 1950.

In 1936 Mr. Bray was initiated as a Bard of the Cornish Gorsedd at Kelly Rounds, Egloshayle, in recognition of his work on local history in the area. He left behind a large collection of ancient stone artefacts, including a fragment of a second cross head from Trequite. The stones are now cared for by Mr. J. Scott for Wadebridge O.C.S.

In recent years the author and other Old Cornwall Society members have re-erected a further three crosses and have encouraged the preservation and erection of several more discoveries. Over the years the skills of the St. Breward stone masons and the generosity of the local granite quarries in supporting the Federation has been outstanding. William Nankivell & Sons Ltd. of Tor Down Quarry provided the base stone and renovated the Three

Hole Cross in Egloshayle parish in 1939. The Middle Moor cross at St. Breward was also re-erected in 1939 by Bodmin O.C.S., who arranged for a stone mason - no doubt a St. Breward man - to cut a new tenon and socket for the monument. The Cornish De Lank Granite Quarries Co. were commissioned by the Wadebridge O.C.S. on three separate occasions under the guidance of their manager Mr. J.W. Coggin. They renovated Trequite Cross in 1947, Job's Cross in 1952, both at St. Kew; and later Penwine Cross, St. Mabyn in 1969. On examination of Job's Cross, the skill of the stonemasons can truly be appreciated. When the monument was discovered only a third of the wheel head existed but today the head is complete and it is difficult to discern which parts are original and which are modern, the restoration having been so well executed.

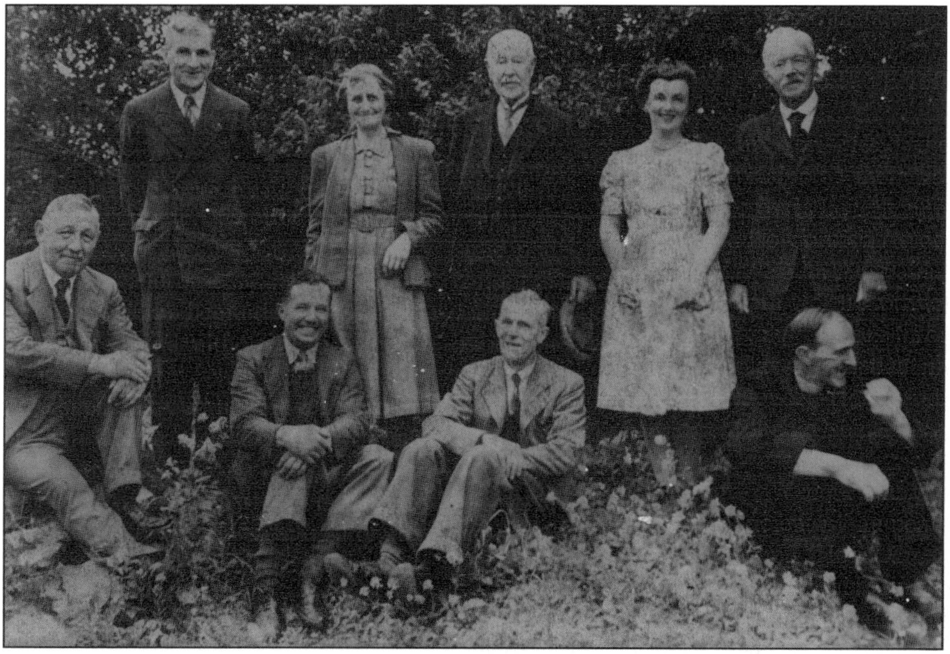

Some of the members of Wadebridge OCS Summer 1947, responsible for re-erecting several crosses in the area
Front Row: Mr. G.H. Gardner, Mr. Bray Jnr. Mr. Stevens, Rev. A. Longden;
Back Row: Mr. A. Barker, Mrs. Stevens, Mr. Nicholas Bray (President); Mrs Lovell, Mr. M. Cleave.

Hantergantick Quarry, which is situated immediately above De Lank, has also been involved with restoration work on stone crosses. In 1983, the Trevia Walls cross from Lanteglos by Camelford was accidentally fractured and removed to the quarry, where it was repaired. In 1987 the quarry received a commission from Truro to lengthen Truro's High Cross from 4 feet (1.2M) to 10 feet (3M). This required removing a large block of granite off the moor, which was of suitable texture to the original monument, cutting a new shaft and fixing the old to the new. Many other crosses and ancient monuments have also been restored over the years by the men of the St. Breward quarries.

Launceston O.C.S. can also boast many achievements in the field of restoration. In 1950 they rescued the Holyway Cross at South Petherwin and had the stone re-erected. Later in 1954 with the assistance of St. Breward quarries, they restored the Laneast churchyard cross to its former glory, and also the Lantern cross at St. Mary Magdalene, Launceston in 1977.

ii Discovering Cornish Crosses

In the past decade several previously unrecorded stone crosses have been discovered throughout the county. Today, with the increase in development within the Duchy, the many road alterations and the changes in agricultural practises, it is possible that many more discoveries will be made. In recent years four crosses have been discovered in use as gateposts; in the parishes of Warbstow in 1973, Menheniot in 1984, Lesnewth in 1987 and Lanlivery in 1990. In addition to this many cross heads and cross fragments have also been found, built into hedges, stiles and property.

To know where to look and what to examine we must first consider the way these ancient monuments were constructed. The majority of wayside crosses, whether wheel headed or Latin, were supported by a base stone. The head and shaft were cut from one piece of stone, usually moorland granite, with a tenon cut at the end of the shaft. The cross base was usually any suitable piece of moorland stone, with a mortice cut in it to receive the tenon. (See Fig. 6). Sometimes these base stones were large boulders already *in situ*, where a mortice was cut on site. In most cases the base stones were trimmed and roughly shaped to suit the monument that they were required to support, i.e. a heavy base stone to support a tall cross. The mortice which is cut in the base stone is usually rectangular and may only be a few inches deep or cut straight through the stone.

The shaft of a granite cross has, in the past, been of great value to farmers and landowners. They have been discovered in use as gateposts, steps of stiles, built into hedges, used as footbridges over mill leats, lintels in buildings, and rubbing posts in fields. The ingenuity of the Cornish to adapt these early Christian relics to more mundane secular purposes appear unlimited.

The base stones were normally of little use, being of irregular size and shape. Their most useful purpose was to block up a hole in a nearby hedge. In many cases the base stones were left *in situ* due to their physical size or pushed up against the nearest hedge and abandoned. Therefore, if we find a base stone of a Cornish cross, we can be reasonably sure that it is either in situ or very near to its original position, marking an ancient track or boundary.

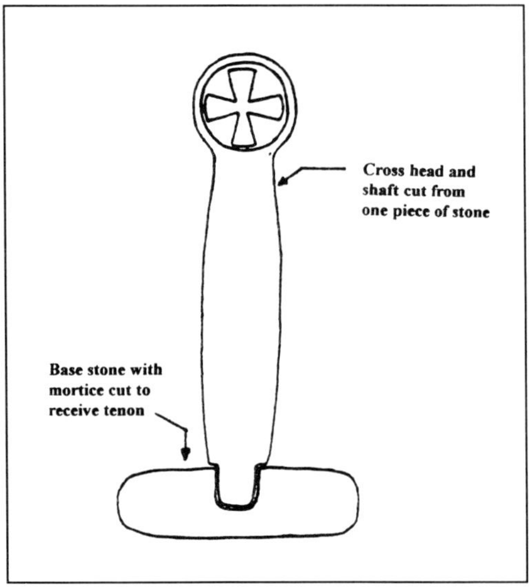

Fig. 6. A Wheel Headed Wayside Cross

WHERE TO LOOK

In 1930 the late Mr Charles Henderson published a paper entitled '*Missing Cornish Crosses*', and listed clues to a further 150 missing monuments, based on documentary evidence and field names. Henderson examined many of the parish Tithe Apportionment Maps and Schedules, which date from between 1838 and 1843, noting all the field names suggesting a possible cross site.

e.g. Messengrouse (Meadow of the Cross) Park-an-Grouse (Field of the Cross)

These field names he believed were certain evidence of a stone cross, but he suggested that the English equivalent "Cross Park" or "Cross Close", found in the east of the county, may only refer to the close proximity to a crossroads or, in fact that a footpath crosses the field.

However, two of our more recent discoveries, St. Wenn in 1989 and Lanlivery in 1990, have been made in fields called "Cross Park", therefore they must not be ruled out. Mary Henderson has continued this research, recording all the known field names connected with the word "cross" within the county, together with the field numbers and acreage.

When endeavouring to find crosses which were set up as boundary stones, it is useful to examine the parish Terriers. These were documents written by the local incumbent reporting to the Bishop about the assets of the parish. The documents were usually set out as an inventory, listing the church plate, property and land and, in many cases, laying down the boundaries of the parish and the glebe. For example, in the 1613 Terrier, the glebe land at the parish of Cardinham was marked by four crosses in the north, east, south and west.

> *" ...... it is bounded on the east with lands in the terrier of George Rawe near adjoining to a crosse called Wydeyeat Crosse, in the west with the lands of the Lords of the Manor of Cardinham adjoininge to a crosse called Peaches Crosse in the north with the lands of the Lords of the Manor of Cardinham adjoining to a crosse called Poundstock Crosse. In the south with the lands of the same adjoining to a crosse called Averies ....".*

Today, two of these crosses still exist, the other two are lost, perhaps waiting to be re-discovered. Documentary evidence of crosses can also be found in old deeds and papers concerning the sale of land where bound stones are frequently mentioned. Estate maps are also a source of field names and clues to crosses, such as the Lanhydrock Atlas; four volumes of maps drawn in 1695 by Joel Gascoyne and today still preserved in Lanhydrock House, Bodmin.

When out walking in the countryside the author keeps a sharp lookout for any stone resembling a cross. Climbing over stiles he examines each step and any surrounding stones, on passing gateways he scrutinises the gateposts, especially when they are close to a boundary or an ancient track. Old farm buildings are also a possibly place to check, especially if there are any records of ancient chapels or holy wells on the site.

iii Viewing the Monuments

When viewing the crosses featured in this guide book, it would aid the visitor to carry an up-to-date Ordnance Survey map of the area, a compass, a waterproof coat and a pair of wellington boots.

The stone crosses of North Cornwall can loosely be divided into four main categories as regard to access:

1. Unlimited public access - crosses beside public roads, tracks and footpaths.
2. Possible restricted access - crosses preserved inside churches or in churchyards.
3. Restricted public access to crosses in private estates and gardens.
4. No public access - where crosses are in private grounds or gardens.

Those crosses on or beside public roads, tracks and footpaths pose few problems to the visitor, although some are beside narrow lanes where parking may present difficulties. It is therefore advisable to park at a more suitable site and walk to the monument, thereby reducing the risk of obstructing other road users or blocking field entrances. When walking public footpaths please respect the landowner's property; do not walk three or four abreast, most paths have a nominal width suitable for two persons to pass. Keep to the defined route and follow the Country Code. If in any doubt as to whether a public right of way exists, make enquiries locally, the majority of farmers and landowners are most helpful if approached.

Some of the crosses featured in this guide are preserved in parish churches, most of which are unlocked during daylight hours. Unfortunately, some are now kept locked due to the growing amount of vandalism and theft. In these cases there is usually the name and address of a local key holder or churchwarden written on the notice board in the church porch; the genuine visitor is always most welcome. A donation towards the church fabric is always appreciated and helps to maintain these ancient buildings for future generations. Many crosses remain preserved in the churchyards, where access is not normally restricted.

There are a few crosses on private estates, where there is limited public access when the grounds and gardens are open to the public. In these cases there is no free access to view the monuments and visitors wishing to see the stones should consult the opening times and charges that apply.

The crosses situated in private grounds are not normally accessible unless a prior arrangement with the owner has been secured. Many of the crosses in Cornwall are listed as Scheduled Ancient Monuments by English Heritage and are therefore protected by law. It is illegal to damage or remove them and being a scheduled ancient monument does not signify that the public have any rights to view them. Many are still in private grounds.

The author has endeavoured to provide an accurate guide for residents and visitors alike, who view these ancient monuments. At the time of printing all site positions and access details are assumed correct, but the author cannot guarantee these details. Sometimes crosses have been shifted due to the sale of land or property, and a development can in some cases necessitate the closing or diversion of a public right of way.

The Country Code

1. Enjoy the countryside and respect its life and work.
2. Guard against all risks of fire.
3. Fasten all gates.
4. Keep dogs under close control.
5. Keep to public paths.
6. Use gates and stiles to cross fences, hedges and walls.
7. Leave livestock, crops and machinery alone.
8. Take all litter home.
9. Do not pollute ponds, streams and rivers.
10. Protect wildlife, plants and trees.
11. Take special care on country roads.
12. Make no unnecessary noise.

3 Gazetteer of Stone Crosses

1	Tresinney Cross	Advent
2	Gothic Cross Head	Bodmin
3	Churchyard Shaft	Bodmin
4	Berry Tower Cross	Bodmin
5	Callywith (Greeditch) Cross	Bodmin
6	Callywith No. 2	Bodmin
7	Carminow Cross	Bodmin
8	Castle Street Hill Cross	Bodmin
9	Berrycombe Cross	Bodmin
10	St. Nicholas No. 1	Bodmin
11	The Whitecross	St Breock
12	Tredinnick Cross	St Breock
13	Cemetery Cross	St Breward
14	Cross Shaft Outside Inn	St Breward
15	Higher Lank No. 1	St. Breward
16	Higher Lank No. 2	St Breward
17	Middle Moor Cross	St Breward
18	Roughtor Cross Base	St Breward
19	Emblance Downs Base	St Breward
20	Basil No. 1	St. Clether
21	Basil No. 2	St Clether
22	Basil No. 3	St Clether
23	New Park Cross	St Clether
24	Tarret Bridge Cross	St Clether
24a	Trefranck Cross	St Clether
25	Holy Well Roof	Davidstow
26	Lambrenny Cross	Davidstow
27	Trevivian No. 1	Davidstow
28	Trevivian Farmhouse	Davidstow
29	Egloshayle Churchyard No 1	Egloshayle
30	Egloshayle Churchyard No 2	Egloshayle
31	The Prior's Cross	Egloshayle
32	The Three Hole Cross	Egloshayle
33	Pencarrow Cross	Egloshayle
34	Trelights Cross Base	St Endellion
35	Longcross	St Endellion
36	Tresungers Cross	St Endellion
37	Penally Terrace Cross	Forrabury
38	Church Path, Forrabury	Forrabury
39	Lancarffe Cross	Helland
40	Anderton Mill Cross	St Juliot
41	St Juliot's Cross	St Juliot
42	Tregatheral Cross	St Juliot
43	Polrode Cross	St Kew
44	Skisdon Cross	St Kew
45	Cross Shaft in Parish Church	St Kew
46	Cross Shaft in Church Tower	St Kew
47	Chapel Amble Cross	St Kew
48	Trequite Cross	St.Kew
49	Trequite Cross Head	St Kew
50	Jobs Cross	St Kew
51	Churchyard Cross	Laneast
52	Laneast Downs Cross	Laneast
53	Tregoodwell Cross	Lanteglos by Camelford
54	Castle Goff Stone	Lanteglos by Camelford
55	Rectory Cross Head	Lanteglos by Camelford
56	Valley Truckle Cross	Lanteglos by Camelford
57	Trewalder Cross	Lanteglos by Camelford
58	Rectory Cross	Lanteglos by Camelford
59	Trevia Walls Cross	Lanteglos by Camelford
60	Trevia Cross	Lanteglos by Camelford
61	Gothic Cross in Churchyard	St Mary M. Launceston
62	Cross Shaft in Churchyard	St Mary M. Launceston
63	Dunheved Cross	St Mary M. Launceston
64	Cross Head at Southgate	St Mary M. Launceston
65	Newport Cross	St Stephen by Launceston
66	Cross in Churchyard	St Thomas by Launceston
67	Treniffle Cross	Lawhitton
68	St Michael's Churchyard	St Michael's Lesnewth
69	Tregrylls Cross	St Michael's Lesnewth
70	Cross Hill	St Mabyn
71	Lane End Cross	St Mabyn
72	Penwine Cross, Longstone	St Mabyn
73	Longstone Cross Base	St Mabyn
74	Tresloggett Cross	St Mabyn
75	Boconnion Cross, Colquite	St Mabyn
76	Cross in Parish Church	Marhamchurch
77	Base Stone in Churchyard	St. Merryn
78	Tresallyn Cross	St. Merryn
79	Trevenning Cross	Michaelstow
80	Churchyard Cross	Michaelstow
81	Trevenning No. 1	Michaelstow
82	Trevenning No. 2	Michaelstow
83	Waterpit Down Cross Shaft	Minster
84	Treglines Cross	St. Minver Highlands
85	St. Enodoc Church	St Minver Highlands
86	St Michael's, Porthilly	St Minver Lowlands
87	Tonacombe Cross	Morwenstow
88	Churchyard Cross Shaft	Padstow
89	Padstow Churchyard Cross	Padstow
90	Prideaux Brune Vault	Padstow
91	Prideaux Place Cross	Padstow
92	Deer Park Cross	Padstow
93	Holyway (Holloway) Cross	South Petherwin
94	Maer Farm Cross	Poughill
95	St. Teath Cross	St. Teath
96	Bosinney/ Fenterleigh Cross	Tintagel
97	Trevena/Trevillet Cross	Tintagel
98	Trevalga Cross	Tintagel
99	Penpol Cross	Tresmeer
100	Cross Fragment	Tresmeer
101	Youlstone No. 1	Warbstow
102	Youlstone No. 2	Warbstow

1

Tresinney Cross
Advent

WHEEL HEADED WAYSIDE CROSS

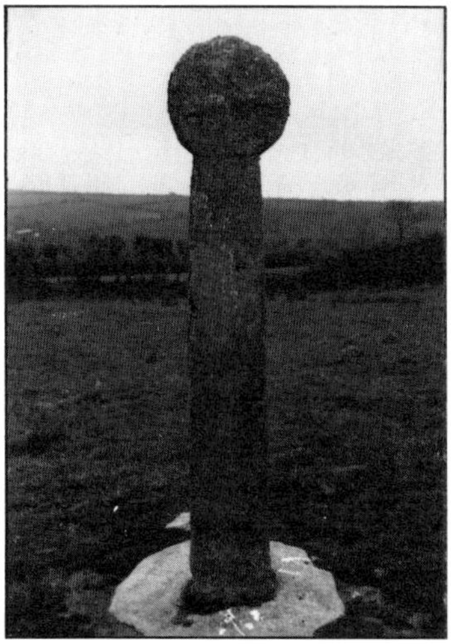

SX 1051, 8124 - On the church path, a quarter of a mile due south of Advent church, which in turn is 1 1/2 miles south of Camelford town. Access - Unlimited (It is on a public footpath).

Tresinney cross still stands *in situ* beside an ancient track from the church towards the farms of Trewint and Steps. The path splits close to the monument, one path leading to each farm. Ellis suggested that the cross may have been connected with a much longer route from Michaelstow, via Tresinney and Watergate, past Lanlivery Rock to Warbstow.

The monument is one of the tallest complete round headed wayside crosses of its type. The sheer weight of the stone has caused it to sink, with its base now in a shallow ditch. The shaft of the cross is slim and has a slight entasis on its sides and the head displays an equal limbed cross in relief with expanded ends, enclosed in a narrow bead. The reverse face is similar.

Height 8' 6" (2.59M), Width of head 1' 9" (0.53M), Width of shaft 11" (at neck) (0.28M), 1' 2" (at its base) (0.35M), Thickness of shaft 8" (0.2M), Base stone approx. 4' in dia. (1.22M), 8 1/2" thick (0.215M)

2

Gothic Cross Head
Bodmin

LANTERN CROSS/RELIQUARY

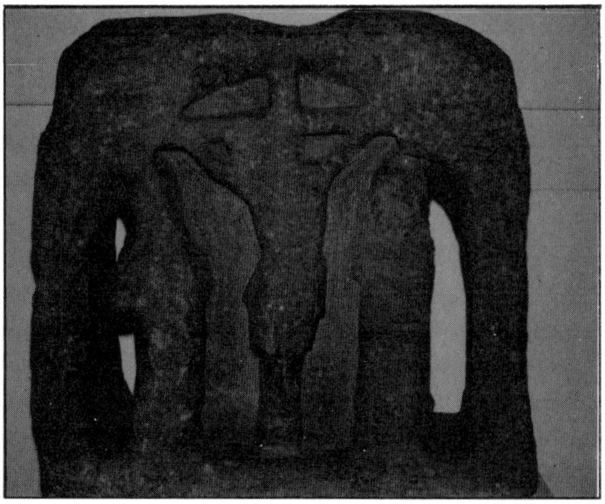

SX 0732, 6704 - Inside St. Petroc's parish church at Bodmin. Access - When the church is open, if locked, the name and address of a key holder is usually written on the notice board in the church porch.

This fine Gothic lantern cross is preserved in St. Petroc's church, at the west end of the building. Maclean suggested that it was probably the churchyard cross and Langdon thought it may have once been set up on the octagonal shaft on the south-west side of the churchyard. (See No. 3 in this guide).

The monument was discovered in the churchyard during the 19th century. It displays a well executed example of the Crucifixion scene, with figures of Our Lord Jesus Christ, St. John and the Virgin Mary, all cut in relief. On the sides of the cross head two single figures are carved, perhaps bishops or saints. The back of the cross head is hollowed out and displays a cable beading around it and was never decorated. Mary Henderson suggests that this recess may have been used for holy relics and notes similarities between this stone and reliquaries at Breage and St. Allen.

Height 1' 5" (0.43M), Width 1' 6" (0.455M), Thickness 4" to 7" (0.1M to 0.18M)

3

Churchyard Shaft
Bodmin

SEMI-GOTHIC CROSS SHAFT

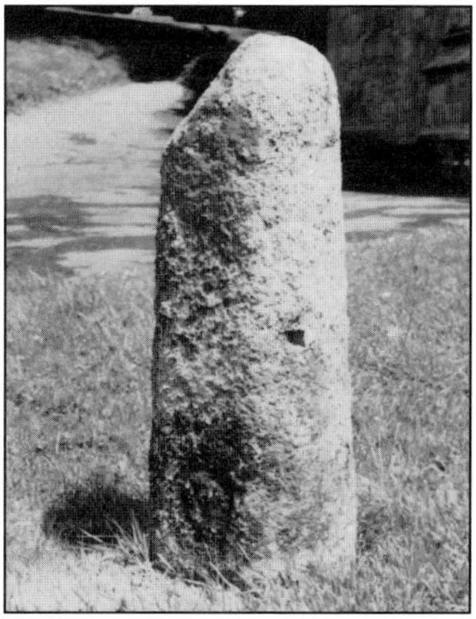

SX 0730, 6703 - The stone stands close to St. Guron's Well in the south-west side of the churchyard. Access - Unlimited.

This badly weathered octagonal shaft was once highly decorated. Maclean recorded that the stone was discovered in use as a hinge post at the door of the well at the Bore, prior to being removed to the churchyard. A hole in the top of the shaft still bears evidence of this use, and no visible remains of the figures and ornamentation illustrated by Iago can be seen today. In a footnote to his sketch of the cross shaft, he records that the stone still possesses a tenon on the lower end. Its base stone was for many years in use as a doorstep to a cottage in Bore Street.

Height 2' 11" (0.89M), Width of shaft (at top) 9" (0.23M), Width of shaft (at bottom) 1' (0.305M)

4

Berry Tower Cross
Bodmin

WHEEL HEADED WAYSIDE CROSS

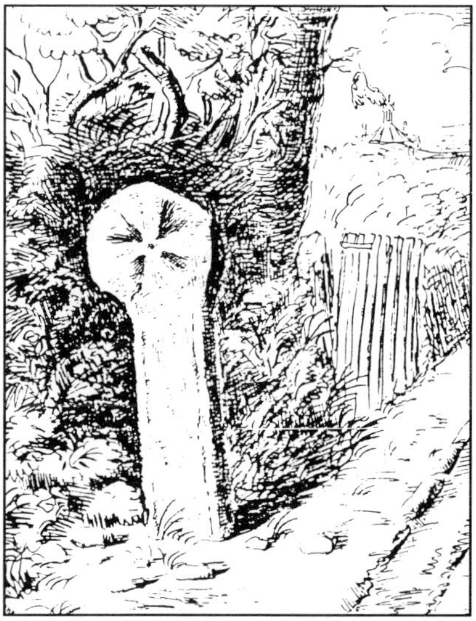

SX 0724, 6746 - This cross stands beside the ruined church tower at the town's cemetery at the top of Berry Hill. Access - Unlimited.

This cross previously stood at the end of Cross Lane, at its junction with the road leading from Bodmin through Clerkenwater to the parish of Helland. It was removed to Berry Tower, its present site, in the year 1860. The tower is all that remains of the Church of the Holy Rood built between 1501 and 1514.

William Iago illustrated the monument before it was moved and his sketch suggests that the cross was once much taller.

The cross head leans considerably to one side and displays a cross with widely expanded limbs on each face, neither of which cross is upright. The head itself is rather mutilated and its shaft carries a narrow beading running down each side. The illustration here was re-produced from the original sketch book of William Iago dated 1873 and shows the monument on Cross Lane.

Height 4' 4" (1.32M), Width of head 1' 6" (0.47M), Width of shaft 1' (0.305M), Thickness 10" (0.255M)

5

Callywith (Greeditch) Cross
Bodmin

WHEEL HEADED BOUNDARY CROSS

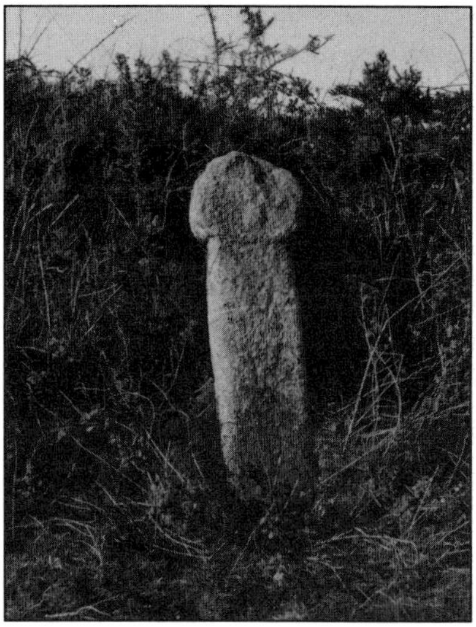

SX 0856, 6795 - Stands against a hedge, close to a bridge which takes a minor road to Callabarrett Farm across the A30 Bodmin by-pass. Access - Unlimited.

This old cross marks the boundary between Cardinham and Bodmin and although the stone is not in its original position, it is thought to be near it. The stone is recorded as being called Greeditch Cross in the 1613 parish Terrier of Cardinham, which set out the Bounds and limits of the parish. It reads *"..... to the forde of a lake called Callywith Lake and so to Greeditch Crosse adjoining to Bodmyn parishe and from thence downward to a place called Parkelane....".* Langdon suggested that the head of the cross is so battered due to the ancient custom of the Beating of the Bounds. The crosses carved on each face are almost worn away, but can be just discerned if viewed in the right light. The ceremony of the Beating of the Bounds still occasionally takes place and was last performed on the 13th April 1994.

During the construction of the Bodmin by-pass the cross was removed to a Council yard for protection. Later in 1977 the monument was re-erected as close as possible to its former site.

Height 5' 4" (1.625M), Width of head 1' 8" (0.51M), Width of shaft 1' 3 1/2" (0.39M), Thickness 9" (0.23M)

6

Callywith No. 2
Bodmin

LATIN CROSS FRAGMENT

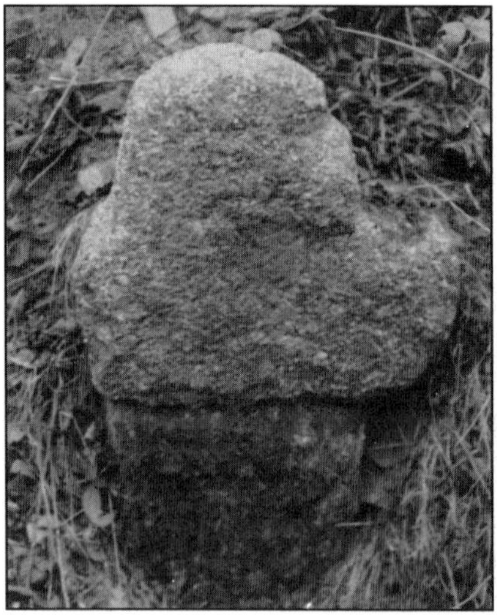

SX 0856, 6795 - Stands next to Callywith (Greeditch) Cross. Access - Unlimited.

In 1975 the Callywith (Greeditch) cross was removed during the construction of the Bodmin by-pass and behind the cross, built into the hedge, was found half of a circular cross base. On removal of the boundary hedge a worked stone was discovered on the Cardinham side of the hedge. It was found to be a fragment of a Latin cross with one arm missing. Later another fragment of granite shaft was found nearby and all these stones were removed by the Cornwall Archaeological Society while the construction work progressed. In 1977 the fragments were joined together and placed close to the original Callywith cross on a new site, as near as possible to its former site.

Height of fragments together 2' 6" (0.76M), Width of head 1' 7 1/2" (0.495M), Width of shaft 1' 1" (0.33M), Thickness 8" (0.2M).

7

Carminow Cross
Bodmin

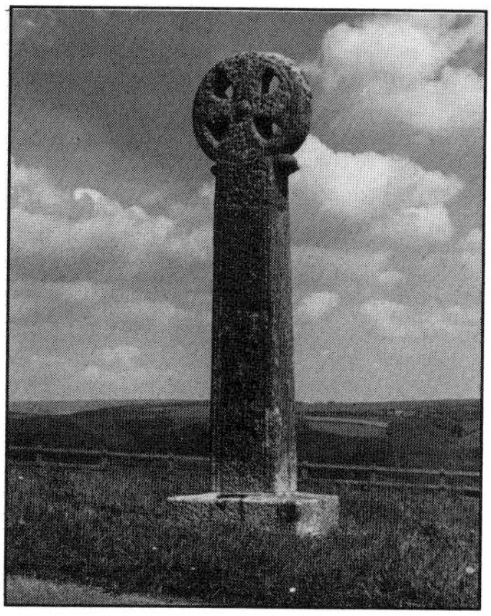

FOUR HOLED BOUNDARY CROSS

SX 0884,6569 - This cross stands in the centre of a roundabout, beside the Bodmin by-pass, 1 1/2 miles S.E. of Bodmin. Access - Unlimited

Blight recorded that this fine four holed cross was partly buried in a ditch at Carminow. When seen by Langdon, he noted that it was in use as a boundary stone between the parishes of Bodmin and Lanhydrock and also suggested that the stone may have originally stood at the crossroads, still known as Carminow Cross. The cross is mentioned as a boundary stone, marking not only the parishes of Bodmin and Lanhydrock but also Cardinham. The bounds and limits of the parish of Cardinham in 1613 read *"and so directly to Carmynowes Crosse - in the S.W. adjoining to Bodmyn and Lanhydrock parishes and from Carmynowes Crosse to a place called Dedlake"*. Today the boundary of Cardinham stops just short of Carminow Cross, having been altered at some time in the past. In 1894 the cross was removed from its former site and re-erected on a large granite shaft and stepped base in its present position. A triangular post was replaced as a boundary stone, marking the former site, and inscribed. *"Bodmin - Former site of Carminow Cross Parish Boundary 1894"*. When the Bodmin by-pass was constructed in 1975 the cross was fenced off for protection until work was completed, and then erected on the nearby new roundabout.

The cross head is the second largest in the county and displays an equal limbed cross with widely splayed limbs enclosed in an outer ring. The outer ring is a perfect circle and consists of a double bead. On one face there are five bosses displayed, one on each limb and one in the centre. The reverse face also displays a central boss and the limbs are decorated by many small sunken holes.

Height of original monument 4' (1.22M), Width of head 2' 11 1/2" (0.9M), Width of shaft 1' 6" (0.455M), Thickness 7" to 1' (0.18M to 0.305M), Total height of renovated monument 12' (3.655M)

8

Castle Street Hill Cross
Bodmin

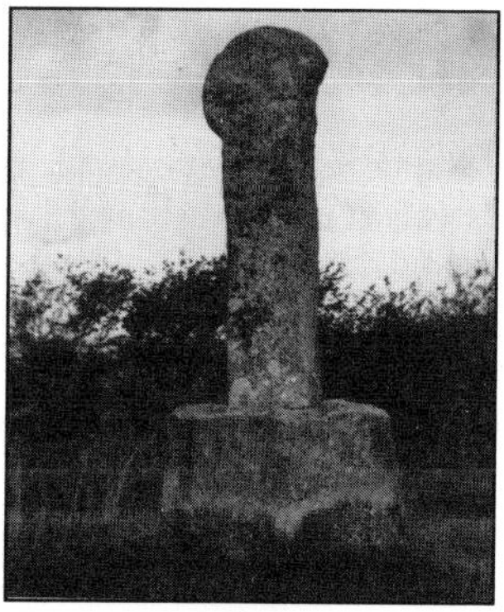

WHEEL HEADED WAYSIDE CROSS

SX 9785, 6754 - Stands beside the roadside at the top of Castle Street Hill, half a mile north-east of the parish church. Access - Unlimited.

Castle Street Hill was originally the main route north out of Bodmin across Bodmin Moor to Launceston, prior to the modern road being constructed through Cooksland. The cross was thrown down in 1827 when a new boundary hedge was built and was later removed by a local landowner and used to cover an open well nearby. Here it remained for many years, until in 1925 it was rescued and re-erected on a large block of granite beside the road. The head of the monument has been fractured on one side, leaving it square with the shaft. Each face displays an equal limbed cross with expanded ends in low relief and enclosed in a bead. The cross on each face has been almost worn away due to the punishment it has withstood in the past.

Height 5' 11" (1.8M), Width of head 2' (0.61M), Width of shaft 1' 4" (0.405M), Thickness 10" (0.255M)

9

Berrycombe Cross
Bodmin

WHEEL HEADED WAYSIDE CROSS

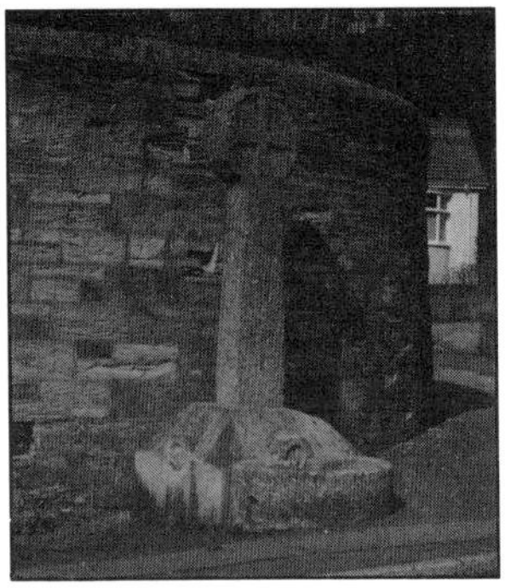

SX 0661, 6741 - Against the eastern boundary wall of the Old Bodmin Gaol at the end of Berrycombe Road. Access - Unlimited.

For many years this round headed cross lay half buried amongst a heap of stones close to the County Gaol, which was re-built in 1850. Langdon later recorded that the cross was re-erected, due to the efforts of Captain Norway R.N. and the Gaol's Visiting Committee. A new base stone was cut incorporating a horse trough and the monument was sited in the middle of the road junction between Scarlet's Well, Cardell, Copshorne and Berrycombe roads.

Although its base stone has never been discovered, Langdon suggested that the stone's original site marking this road junction was probable.

Here it stood until 1968, when a lorry ran out of control down Cardell Road and demolished the cross. It was broken into three pieces and later removed to De Lank granite quarries at St. Breward for restoration. In the autumn of 1973, the renovation of the stone complete, it was replaced against the Gaol wall in its present position.

The cross itself is plain It displays an equal limbed cross with narrow limbs on each face, enclosed by a bead. The shaft is narrow at the neck, emphasising the entasis and provides a well proportioned monument.

Height (above base stone) 7' 2" (2.185M), Width of head 2' 4" (0.71M), Width of shaft (at neck) 1' 1" (0.33M), Width of shaft (at base) 1' 6" (0.46M), Thickness 9 1/2" (0.24M).

10

St. Nicholas No. 1
Bodmin

WHEEL HEADED WAYSIDE CROSS

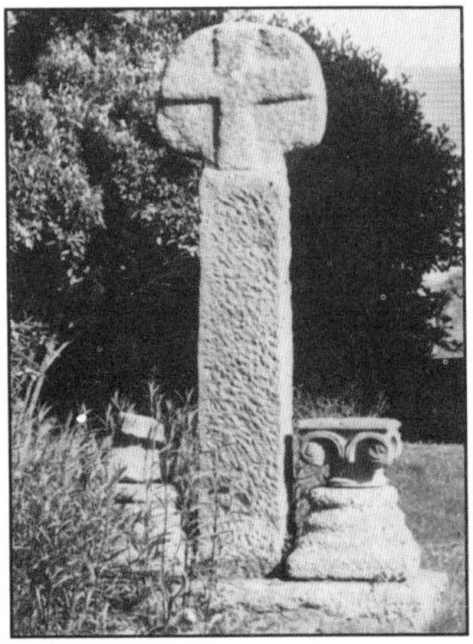

SX 0570, 6658 - In the garden of Pendrea House on Westheath Avenue, opposite the grounds of St. Lawrence Hospital. Access - There is no public access, the cross is on private ground but can easily be seen from the public pavement.

Langdon first recorded this cross at St. Nicholas House in Bodmin in 1902, formerly the home of Mr. Collins. In 1940 the cross head was found by Mr. J. S. Henwood of Pendrea along with other ecclesiastic stones in the grounds of St. Nicholas and later removed to Pendrea. Here it was set up on a modern granite shaft on the lawn in front of the house.

Mr. Collins, who was a great collector of antiquities, left crosses at other properties including two at Higher Lank, St. Breward. It is therefore quite probable that the cross head was removed from the St. Breward area. Henderson recorded that it came from Deaconstow in St. Breward but did not mention the source of his information.

On the front and back of the stone is carved a simple cross in bold relief, the limbs being square and extending to the edge of the monument. The head is round at the top, but has been cut away below the horizontal limbs; no remains of the shaft exist. Recently in 1989 the property at Pendrea House has been extended and the cross re-sited by the boundary hedge of the property

Total height of monument 6' 2 1/2" (1.89M), Height 1' 7" (0.48M), Width of head 1' 10" (0.56M), Thickness 5" (0.128M).

The Whitecross
St. Breock

WHEEL HEADED WAYSIDE CROSS

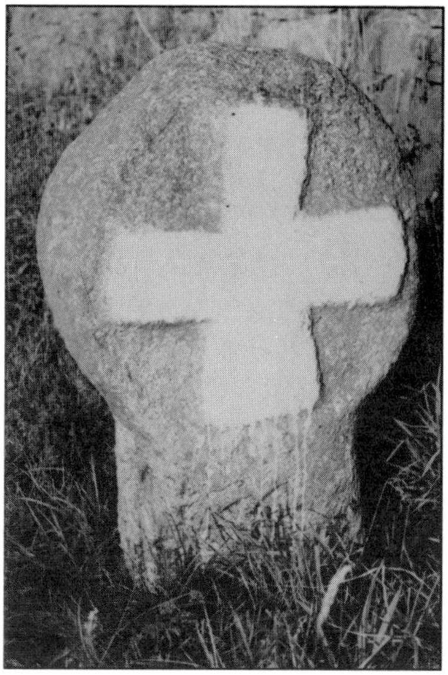

SW 9645, 7201 - On the western side of a crossroads, in the village of Whitecross on the A39 Wadebridge to St. Columb Major road. Access - Unlimited.

There are five villages in Cornwall known as Whitecross; the only other which still boasts a stone cross is in the parish of Ludgvan and stands beside the main A30 trunk road to Penzance.

This stone, which stands on the grass verge near the Royal Cornwall Agricultural Showground, displays an equal limbed cross in relief with expanded ends on each face, both of which are whitewashed.

The shaft was fractured prior to 1858 and later clamped together by a local blacksmith. This repair lasted over 100 years, but during recent years became loose. The ground level has also risen over the last century and the cross has remained buried up to its neck in soil.

The author became concerned about vehicles mounting the grass verge and parking close to the monument which, being loose, he considered vulnerable to theft or damage.

In 1994 a restoration project for the cross was organised by Mr. David Attwell of the North Cornwall Heritage Coast & Countryside Service, in conjunction with several other bodies and was overseen by Ann Preston-Jones, Field Monument Warden for English Heritage. In December 1994 the monument was dug up and restored by Somerset conservators, Sue and Lawrence Kelland, on the grounds of the nearby Showground. A new granite base stone was supplied by St. Breward stonemason, Mr. Noel Hill, while the two portions of cross shaft were pinned together by the conservators using phosphor bronze pins. On completion the monument was cleaned and its cross in relief was re-painted using traditional lime-wash.

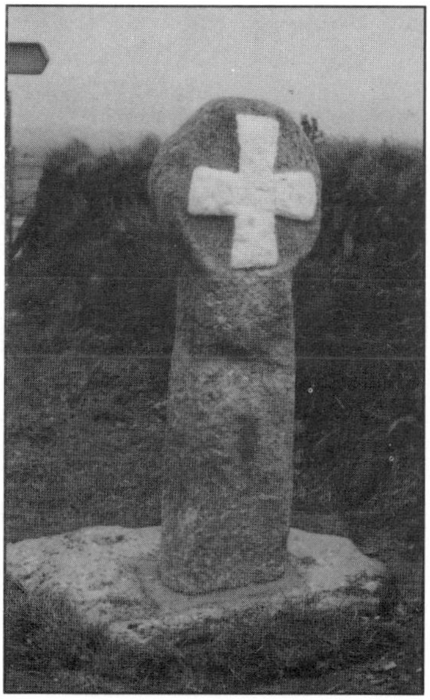

The monument was recorded by Blight in 1858 as being 4 ft 2 ins in height, but in recent years measured only 2 ft 6 ins. No tenon or base stone was discovered, although most of the shaft remained and has now been set up at almost its full height. An Ordnance Survey bench mark was found cut on the eastern side of the shaft. The monument now stands out more prominently beside the A.39 road, but still retains its former site. The cross probably originally marked a churchpath which once crossed the showground en-route to the parish church. It may also have a connection with the ecclesiastical manor of Pawton which was sited one mile south of the monument.

Total height including new shaft 5' 9" 1/2" (1.765M), Height 4' 8" (1.422M), Width of head 1' 8" (0.508M), Width of shaft 1' to 1' 2" (0.305M to 0.355M), Thickness 9" to 10 1/2" (0.229M to 0.267M).

12

Tredinick Cross
St. Breock
ORIGINALLY A WHEEL HEADED CROSS

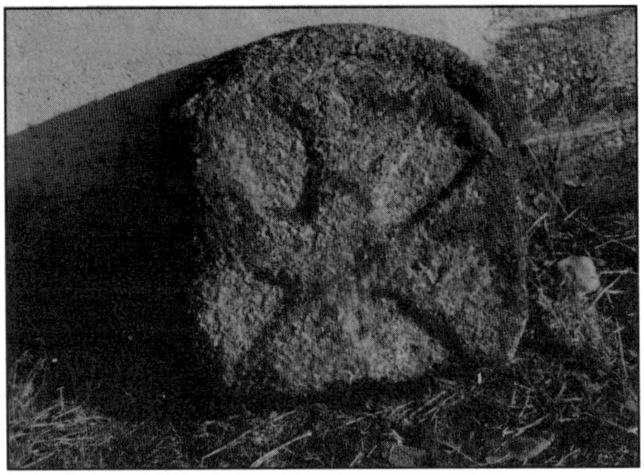

SW 9725, 7213 - At the Tredinick Farmhouse, on the Royal Cornwall Agricultural Showground. The Showground is adjacent to the A39 Wadebridge to St. Columb Major road, one mile from Wadebridge. Access - The monument is on private ground, there is no public access.

The author was made aware of the existence of this cross head in 1987. The rectangular block of granite displays a widely expanded Maltese style cross in relief. Unfortunately, what may have originally been a round headed stone has been 'squared off' erasing parts of the lower and horizontal limbs. Above the upper limb a narrow bead can just be perceived, helping to support the author's theory that the stone was once round headed. An unusual feature is that the stone is worked only on one face, which may suggest that the monument was placed against a wall or hedge where the reverse face was unimportant. The cross head may have been a guide post on one of the numerous footpaths which lead from the outlying farms to St. Breock Church.

The cross head has recently been built into the east wall of the old Tredinick Farmhouse (now known as Boscawen House) for preservation; it had until this time been used as a prop to gates on the Showground.

Height 1' 8" (0.51M), Width of head 1' 9" (0.53M), Thickness 8 1/2" (0.22M)

13

Cemetery Cross
St. Breward
FOUR HOLED CHURCHYARD CROSS

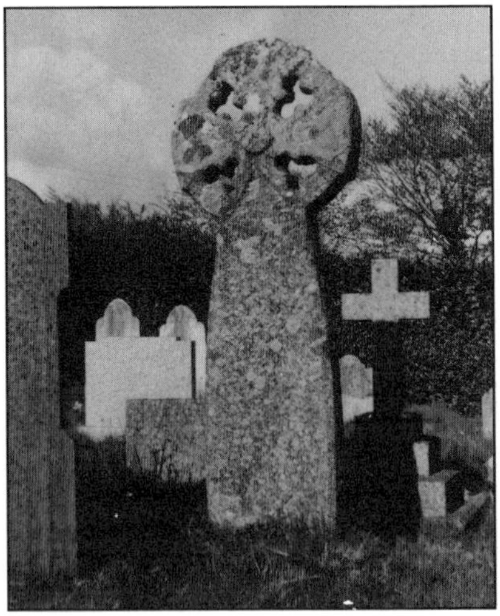

SX 0975, 7730 - In the cemetery adjoining the south side of St. Breward churchyard. St Breward is 8 miles north of Bodmin. Access - Unlimited.

Blight and Langdon illustrated this fragment of a four holed cross straddling the wall which divided the boys' and girls' playgrounds at St. Breward School. Prior to 1853 the cross fragment was sitting on the churchyard wall, which gives credence to the assumption that it is the original churchyard cross. When surveyed in the 1890s the stone had already been renovated on a large granite shaft and removed to the new cemetery.

On the front of the head is a central boss with triquetra knots on each of the three remaining limbs. The limbs are joined by an outer ring, forming a four holed cross, the holes being trefoil in shape due to the cusps. The reverse face does not display any central boss and remains plain in the centre.

Width of cross head fragment 2' 6" (0.76M), Thickness 9" (0.23M), Total height (with new shaft) 7' 2" (2.185M)

14

Cross Shaft Outside Inn
St. Breward
SHAFT OF CHURCHYARD CROSS

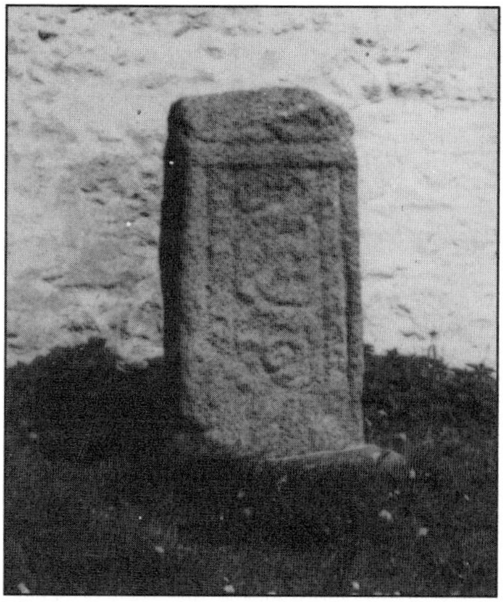

SX 0970, 7728 - Outside the Old Inn at St. Breward churchtown. Access - Unlimited, can be viewed from public road.

This fragment of cross shaft was discovered in use as a building stone in the walls of an outbuilding at the Old Inn, St. Breward. It is assumed, due to its decoration, to be another part of the original churchyard cross and in 1952, when the outbuilding was demolished, it was set up outside the Inn on a granite base stone. Unfortunately the stone is much weathered and today the decoration is difficult to distinguish.

Ellis recorded that the stone displayed a type of vine scroll within a panel with a wide bead running down each side. This type of decoration is common on Northumbrian crosses, although a particularly fine example exists on a cross inside the church at Penally in Pembrokeshire. There have been numerous reports over the years of further fragments of this monument built into walls, although no positive identification has been made.

Height 3' (0.915M), Width between 1' 5" (0.43M) and 1' 8" (0.51M), Thickness 8" (0.2M).

15

Higher Lank No. 1
St. Breward
WHEEL HEADED WAYSIDE CROSS

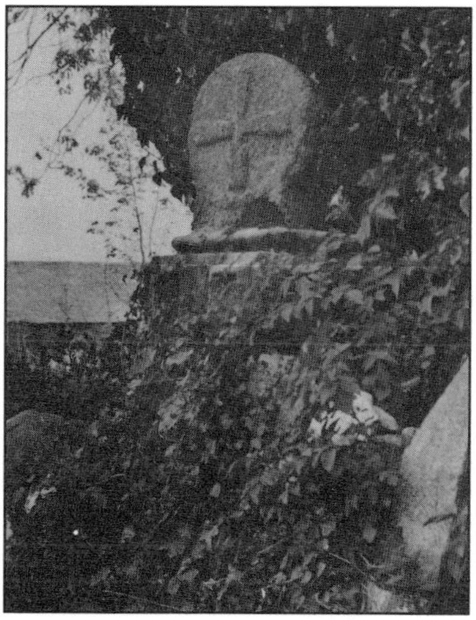

SX 0892, 7562 - In the front garden of Higher Lank Farmhouse, which is 1 1/2 miles south-west of St. Breward churchtown. Access - The monument is on private grounds, there is no public access.

Maclean recorded that this cross head was formerly built into the gable of the farmhouse at Higher Lank. The property was owned by Mr. William Collins in 1813, who was a keen collector of antiquities. Unfortunately Mr. Collins left no records about from where or when he removed crosses, although there are three empty cross bases existing in the parish, which may provide a clue. Today this cross still sits on the rockery, as seen by Langdon prior to publishing his book in 1896. The cross head is elliptical in shape and displays a narrow equal limbed cross with expanded ends enclosed in a fine bead. The reverse face is similar.

Height 1' 8 1/2" (0.52M), Width of shaft 1' 1" (0.33M), Width of head 1' 5 1/2" (0.44M), Thickness 5" (0.127M).

16

Higher Lank No. 2
St. Breward
WHEEL HEADED WAYSIDE CROSS

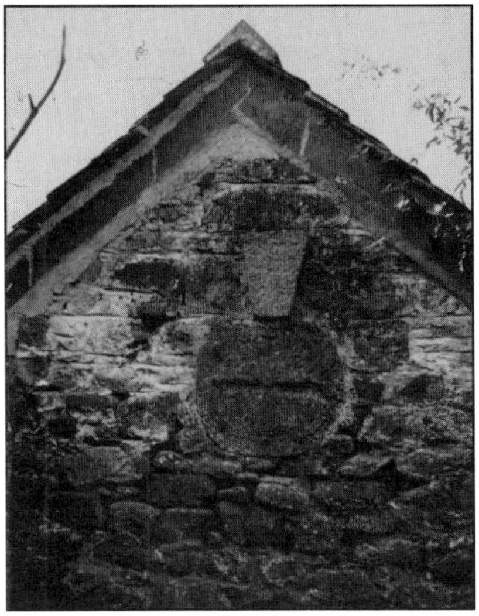

SX 0893, 7562 - Higher Lank Farmhouse is situated 1 1/2 miles south-west of St. Breward. Access - The monument is on private grounds, there is no public access.

This small elliptical cross head eluded Langdon when he visited Higher Lank and surveyed the cross on the rockery (Higher Lank No. 1). It is built into the gable wall of an outbuilding adjoining the farmhouse. The stone is different in design to the cross on the rockery, as it displays a widely incised equal limbed cross, whereas the latter is cut in relief. All the previous history relating to this stone is unknown.

Height 1' 3 1/2" (0.395M), Width 1' 5" (0.43M), Thickness unknown.

17

Middle Moor Cross
St. Breward
WHEEL HEADED WAYSIDE CROSS

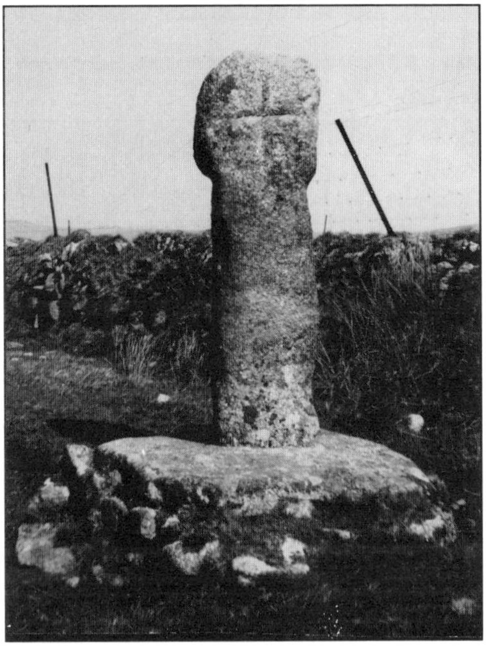

SX 1250, 7930 - The cross is situated near Camperdown Farm, 2 1/2 miles north-east of St. Breward churchtown, on Bodmin Moor. Access - Unlimited.

Sometimes known as the 'Mid Moor Post', this cross stands *in situ* beside an ancient track and acts as a guidepost marking a route across the moors. When illustrated by Maclean in 1873, it was recumbent but was later re-erected by the local vicar Dr. George Martin in 1888. By the year 1938 it had again been knocked over, fracturing the tenon of the cross. This was reported to Bodmin Old Cornwall Society which, with the assistance of St. Breward stone masons, had the monument re-erected again. A new tenon was cut on the bottom of the shaft reducing the stone's height by a foot and the mortice in the base stone enlarged to receive it.

Langdon recorded that there was a legend in the neighbourhood that whenever the cross heard the bells of "Semmenward" (St. Breward) ring, it turned round and round and eventually fell down. The monument is crudely fashioned with a simple incised cross carved on each face, suggesting an early date.

Height 5' 6" (1.675M), Width of head 1' 7 1/2" (0.495M), Width of shaft (at neck) 1' 3" (0.38M), Width of shaft (at base) 1' 5 1/2" (0.445M), Thickness 8" (0.2M), Base stone approx. 4' square (1.22M square).

18

Roughtor Cross Base St. Breward

BASE OF WAYSIDE CROSS

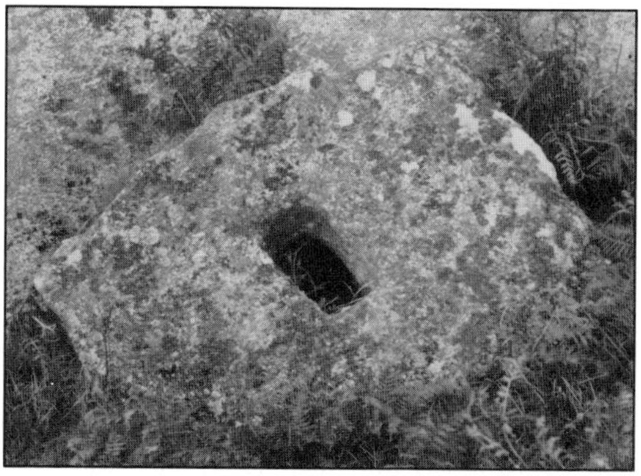

SX 1442, 8049 - On the south-western slopes of Roughtor, on Bodmin Moor. Access - Unlimited.

On the 2 1/2 inch Ordnance Survey map this stone is marked as *"Stone Cross remains of "*, but on visiting Roughtor the visitor will soon realise that finding the stone is not so easy. Roughtor is covered in large granite stones and finding one stone out of thousands proves very difficult. Mary Henderson made several attempts to discover the stone, without success, but later Mr. N. Quinnell of the Ordnance Survey Archaeological section found the cross base and sent her photographs of its location.

The author after unsuccessful searches, borrowed these photographs and eventually found the cross base leaning up against a massive boulder near the foot of the tor. The base stone probably marked a route around Roughtor connecting with the track to Trevillian's Gate and eventually Warbstow.

Length 4' (1.22M), Width 3' 2" (0.965M), Thickness 7 1/2" (0.19M), Mortice 11 3/4" by 6 1/2" (0.3M by 0.165M).

19

Emblance Downs Cross Base St. Breward

BASE OF WAYSIDE CROSS

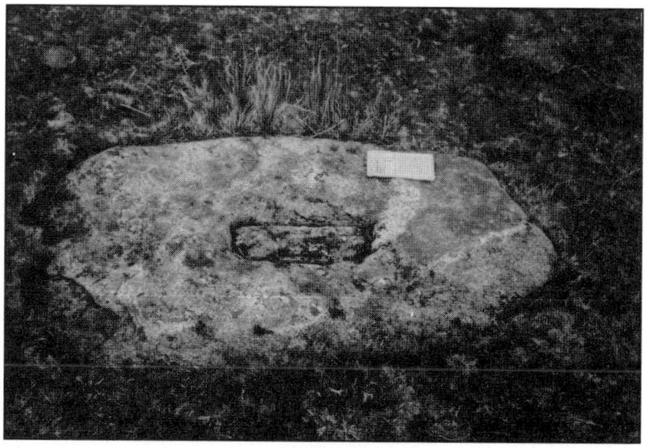

SX 1281, 7764 - Lies on the ground half a mile south-east of Middle Candra Farm, on a track that leads to King Arthur's Hall earthworks. Access - Unlimited.

This cross base lies *in situ* at the intersection of two ancient tracks on Emblance Downs, 1 3/4 miles due east of St. Breward churchtown. Here a track leads from Middle Candra via King Arthur's Hall, skirting the bottom of Garrow Tor and appears to terminate at Wheal Rosa near Butter's Tor. The other track leads south through Bolatherick to Bradford in Blisland parish.

The cross base will be seen between the corner of the last enclosed field and King Arthur's Hall on the open moor. Mary Henderson noted that in 1888 an excursion to the earthworks recorded seeing a cross shaft near this site. A second report of a fragment of a weathered Celtic cross was noted in a book as late as 1948, although today only the cross base remains.

Length 5' 3" (1.6M), Width 3' 5" (1.04M), Thickness 7 1/2" (0.19M), Mortice length 1' 5 1/2" (0.445M), Mortice width 7" (0.178M).

20

Basil No. 1 (By River Inney) St. Clether

WHEEL HEADED WAYSIDE CROSS

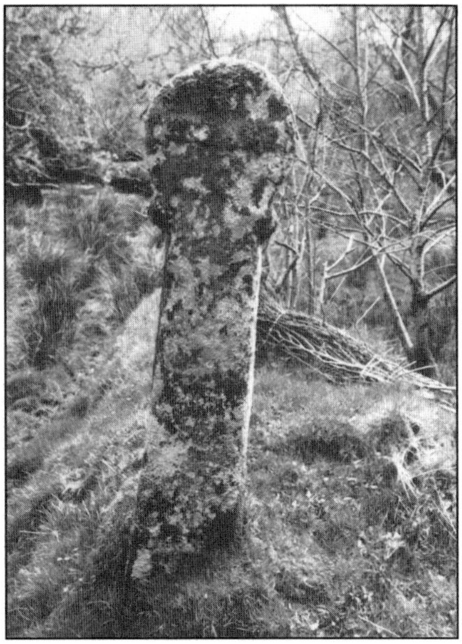

SX 2053, 8418 - St. Clether Church is situated 9 miles west of Launceston and the cross stands a 1/4 mile due south from this church. Access - The cross is on private ground, but can be viewed from the public road at a distance.

This large monolith stands *in situ* on the southern bank of the River Inney, close to the water's edge. It leans considerably to one side, still supported by its base stone. It displays an equal limbed cross with expanded ends on each face and was originally enclosed by a bead around the head, which is now almost worn away. At the neck can be seen the characteristic projections found on all the crosses which were originally on the Barton of Basil.

The cross may have once marked a safe fording place across the river, prior to the road bridge being built. A footpath still survives from Altarnun parish to St. Clether church via Basil Farmhouse, where the river would be forded at the cross.

Height 7' 1" (2.16M), Width of head 2' 1" (0.635M), Width of shaft (at neck) 1' 5" (0.43M), Width of shaft (at base) 1' 7" (0.48M), Thickness (at neck) 6 1/2" (0.165M), Thickness (at base) 8" (0.2M).

21

Basil No. 2 (Near Basil Farmhouse) St. Clether

WHEEL HEADED WAYSIDE CROSS

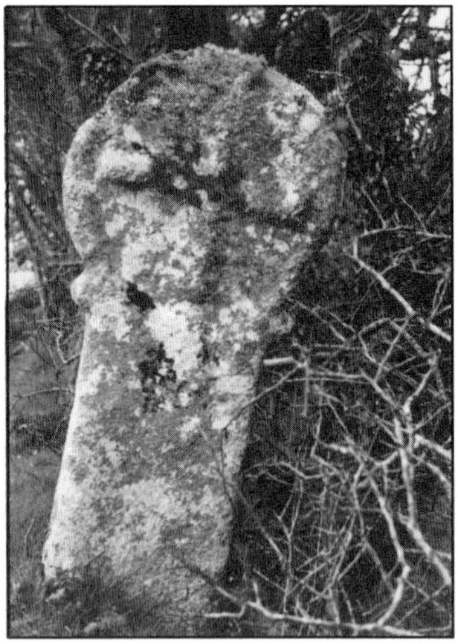

SX 2022, 8420 - Beside the roadside, a 1/4 mile west of Lower Basil Farm. Access - Unlimited.

This cross stands high up on a hedge on the road leading from Basil Farmhouse (formerly known as Lower Basil), west towards Trevillian's Gate. The monument is sheltered by trees and is well camouflaged in the spring and summer months. The cross is very similar in character to Basil No. 1, (see No. 20 in this guide) but shorter with smaller projections and although it is not *in situ* it was undoubtedly connected with Basil No. 1, marking a track to St. Clether church.

Height 5' (1.525M), Width of head 2' (0.61M), Width of shaft (at neck) 1' 6" (0.455M), Width of shaft (at base) 1' 7" (0.485M), Thickness of shaft (at neck) 7 1/2" (0.19M), Thickness of shaft (at base) 9 1/2" (0.24M).

22

Basil No. 3 (Cross-Gates) St. Clether

WHEEL HEADED WAYSIDE CROSS

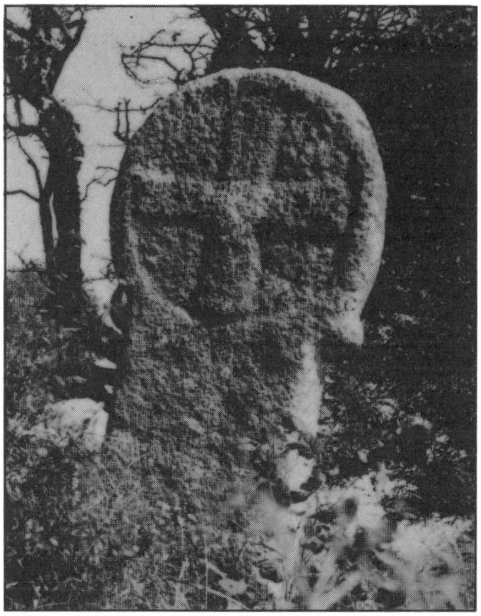

SX 1888, 8402 - This cross stands 1 1/4 miles west of Basil No. 2 at a crossroads known as Cross Gates. Access - Unlimited.

This cross has been re-erected for preservation high up on the edge overlooking the crossroads. Here at a crossroads, the road to Trevillian's Gate is dissected by a road from Hallworthy to Altarnun. Although the stone's original position is unknown, it is assumed that it stood at this intersection and was associated with the Basil No. 2 cross (see No. 21 in this guide), marking the ancient road from Davidstow to St. Clether. Ellis recorded that the similarity between this monument and the other Basil crosses led him to suggest that they were all cut by the same hand.

Height 5' (1.525M), Width of head 2' 2" (0.66M), Width of shaft 1' 6" (0.46M), Thickness 5 1/2" (0.14M).

23

New Park Cross St. Clether

WHEEL HEADED WAYSIDE CROSS

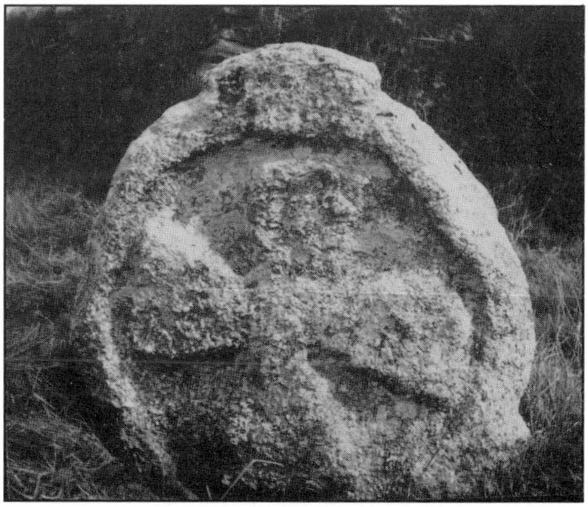

SX 1714, 8371 - The cross is situated 1/4 mile south-west of Trevillians Gate, the parish boundary between Davidstow and St. Clether. Access - Unlimited.

Langdon noted that he first discovered this massive cross head lying at the foot of Roughtor and recorded that in 1885 the stone was removed to its present site. Originally the cross would have marked an ancient track, skirting the tors, and probably connecting with other tracks near Trevillians Gate.

The cross head itself is the largest of the St. Clether crosses and has a projection at the top of the head as well as at the neck of the monument. A projection at the top of the cross is unusual, although some crosses in the Blisland area boast this characteristic such as St. Pratts Cross (East Cornwall No. 17). The cross also displays an equal limbed cross with expanded ends and is cut in high relief, the reverse face is similar.

Height 2' 11" (0.89M), Height of head 2' 7" (0.79M), Width of head 1' 9 1/2" (0.545M), Thickness 10" (0.255M).

24

Tarret Bridge Cross
St. Clether

WHEEL HEADED WAYSIDE CROSS

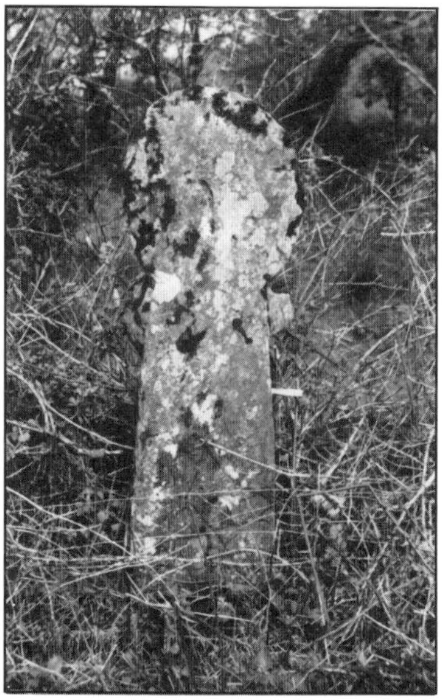

SX 1951, 8495 - Half a mile east of Ta Mill on the minor road between Trevivian and St. Clether. Access - The cross is on private land, but can be viewed from the roadside or nearby footpath.

This Cornish cross is unique, having been cut from slate stone rather than granite; it is the only slate cross in the county known to exist.

Prior to 1893, it formed part of a stone bank along the river Inney, being built horizontally into the hedge at a low level. It was eventually removed and re-erected in its present site by Mr. E. Venning, the former owner of Basil Estate. Its original site has not been established, although it undoubtedly marked the footpath to St. Clether church and holy well which meets the road on the opposite bank of the river. The cross may have also indicated a safe fording place across the river.

Today the head of the cross is very worn, due perhaps to having been washed by the river during flood conditions for many years. One face is completely devoid of any markings, the other, although damaged, does still show evidence of the lower and horizontal limbs. The monument still resembles the other St. Clether crosses, having the usual projections at the neck, but Ellis suggests may be of slightly later date.

Height 5' 8" (1.73M), Width of head 1' 8" (0.51M), Width of shaft (at neck) 1' 2" (0.353M), Width of shaft (at base) 1' 4" (0.41M), Thickness 6 1/2" (0.165M).

24A

Trefranck Cross
St Clether

WHEEL HEADED WAYSIDE CROSS

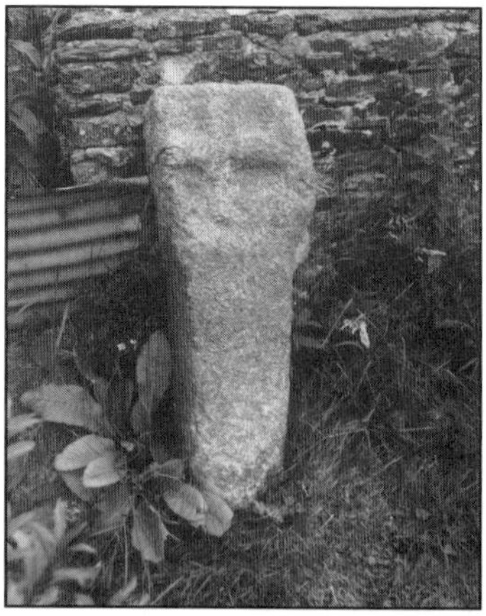

SX 2043, 8492 - The cross is situated at Trefranck Farm, 1/2 mile north of St. Clether church. Access - At present the monument is not accessible to the public.

This mutilated granite cross was discovered in 1993 when a section of hedge was removed to accommodate a new oil tank in the farmhouse grounds. The monument appears to have been used as a simple building stone in the past, having been laterally trimmed down both sides and across its head.

The head originally displayed an equal limbed cross on either face and was enclosed in a bead. At the neck of the monument there is still to be seen one projection; a characteristic seen on all the remaining St. Clether crosses. The author considers that the cross may have originally marked a route from the parish of Treneglos, via Cold Northcott south through Trefranck to the parish church. He hopes that in the future this monument will be restored and re-erected.

Height 2' 11 1/2" (0.902M), Width of existing head 1' 1" (0.33M), Width of shaft 9" (0.229M), Thickness 7 1/2" (0.19M).

25

Holy Well Roof
Davidstow
BASE OF WAYSIDE CROSS

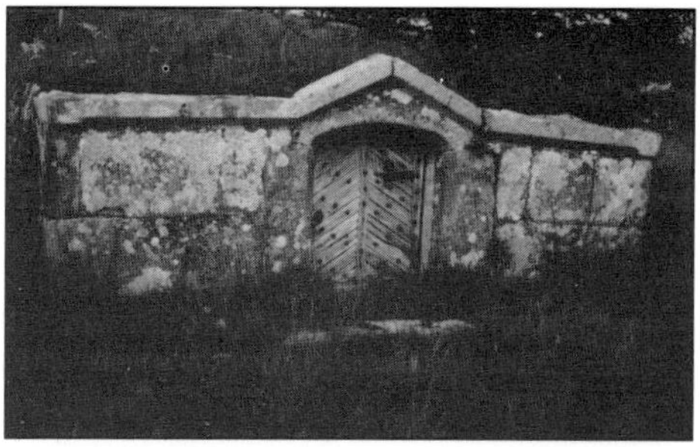

SX 1517, 8737 - The cross base is built into the roof of Davidstow holy well, which is situated in a meadow on the eastern side of the churchyard. Access - A public footpath to the holy well exists.

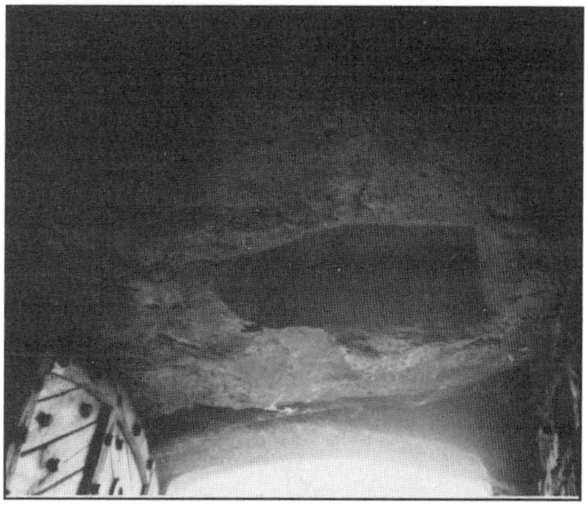

The holy well was renovated in the last century with pieces of stone removed from St. Austen's Well in the adjoining parish of Lesnewth. Above the oak studded door can be seen an inscription which reads *RESTORED M.W. OCTr 1871*. The M.W. are the initials of Michael Williams who restored the well, it has since been restored again during Autumn 1996. When the door is open it is possible to examine the large base stone which must have once supported a large monument. The remainder of the building is covered in a turf bank, and it is not known whether the cross base was brought from Lesnewth or if it originated near the well.

Length 4' 6" (1.37M), Width 4' 1" (1.24M), Thickness 5" to 10" (0.13M to 0.25M), Mortice 1' by 1' 8" (0.305M by 0.51M)

26

Lambrenny Cross
Davidstow
LATIN WAYSIDE CROSS

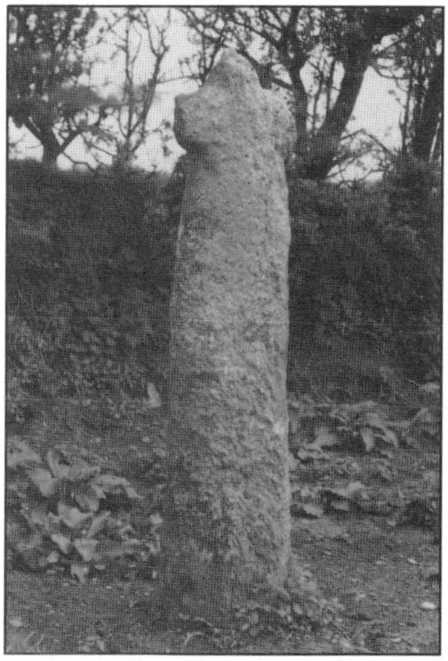

SX 1756, 8677 - The cross stands beside the farm drive to Lambrenny Farm, which was once part of the old church path. Access - Unlimited, the cross stands on a public footpath.

In the past it is believed that the site of this old mutilated cross had been used for private prayer and it was the path which was used to carry the dead to the church for burial from Lambrenny.

The stone is a crudely executed monolith which is almost round in section and tapers upwards to the stunted limbs of the head. These limbs appear to have seen considerable damage over the centuries, although all the edges have been rounded by weathering. Ellis suggested that the stone was bruised into shape with a wooden instrument and not cut with metal tools.

The cross is considered to be *in situ*, although no base stone exists. There are two more similar Latin crosses in Cornwall; one on a footpath to the south of Madron church and known as Boscathnoe Cross and another called Godolphin Cross which stands beside Godolphin church.

Height 5' (1.525M), Width of head 1' 1" (0.33M), Width of shaft (at neck) 9" (0.23M), Width of shaft (bottom) 1' 2 1/2" (0.37M), Thickness 10 1/2" (0.265M).

27

Trevivian No. 1
Davidstow
WHEEL HEADED WAYSIDE CROSS

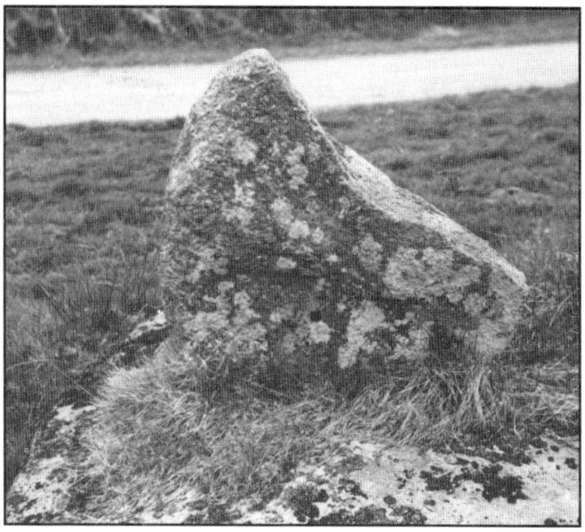

SX 1690, 8524 - This mutilated cross head is situated 1 mile south of the Lambrenny Cross. It stands on a wide grass verge on a minor road leading south-west from Trevivian village. Access - Unlimited.

This cross head is typical of many in the Camelford/St.Clether area, boasting projections at the neck of the monument. Unfortunately earlier this century the cross was damaged, losing almost a third of its head. The stone originally displayed an equal limbed cross with slightly expanded ends in relief on both sides. Ellis was of the opinion that the stone was set up as a supplementary marker to a chain of crosses from Michaelstow via Roughtor and Trevillian's Gate to Warbstow. Considering the size of the base stone, the monument may have originally been tall.

Height 2' 1" (0.63M), Width of head 1' 10" (0.56M), Thickness 6" to 7" (0.15M to 0.18M), Base stone 4' 11" by 3' 6" (1.5M by 1.07M).

28

Trevivian Farmhouse
Davidstow
WHEEL HEADED

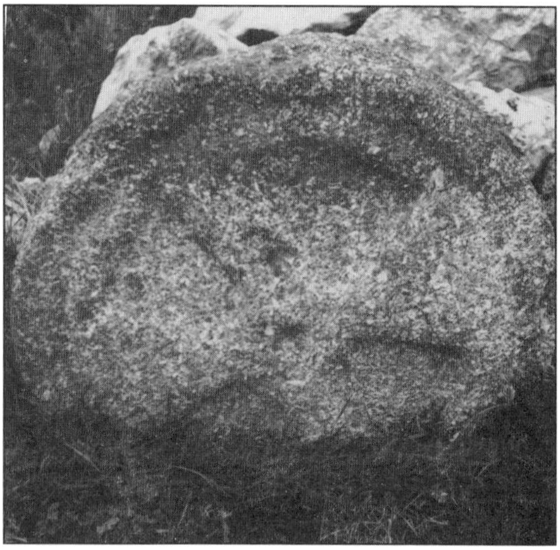

SX 1728, 8535 - On a grass verge outside a farmhouse at Trevivian, a hamlet 2 1/2 miles south-east of the parish church. Access - Although the grass verge may be private, the stone can be easily viewed from the public road.

This carved stone was discovered in 1957 in a nearby field, it was later rescued and placed near the farmhouse. Although it is partially hidden by soil it will be seen that the cross is formed by four triangular sinkings which are enclosed in a bead. The reverse face gives the appearance of being a cheese press and this poses the question as to whether the cross head is authentic.

Height (above ground) 1' 8" (0.51M), Width of head 2' 3" (0.69M), Thickness 7" to 10" (0.18M to 0.26M).

29

Egloshayle Churchyard No. 1
Egloshayle
WHEEL HEADED WAYSIDE CROSS

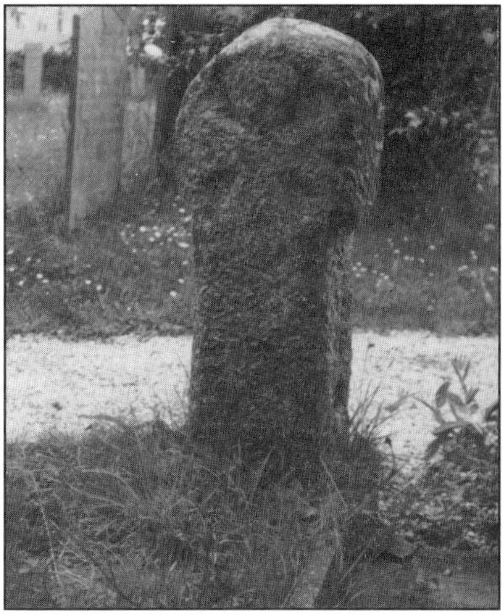

SX 0008, 7197 - Right hand side of south porch, Egloshayle church. The church is situated close to the A389 Wadebridge to Bodmin road, 1 mile from Wadebridge town. Access - Unlimited.

This small cross was discovered in Dunmere Woods near Bodmin and removed to the churchyard for preservation. It displays an equal limbed cross of Greek style in relief on each face. The tell-tale scars of its past existence as a gatepost are much in evidence, with drillings still visible on the shaft. This cross formerly stood on the north side of the churchyard along with Egloshayle No. 2 (see No. 30 in this guide) and they were shifted earlier this century to their present positions.

Height 2' 6 1/2" (0.775M), Width of head 1' 1/2" (0.318M), Width of shaft 10" (0.254M), Thickness 7 1/2" (0.19M)

30

Egloshayle Churchyard No. 2
Egloshayle
WHEEL HEADED WAYSIDE CROSS

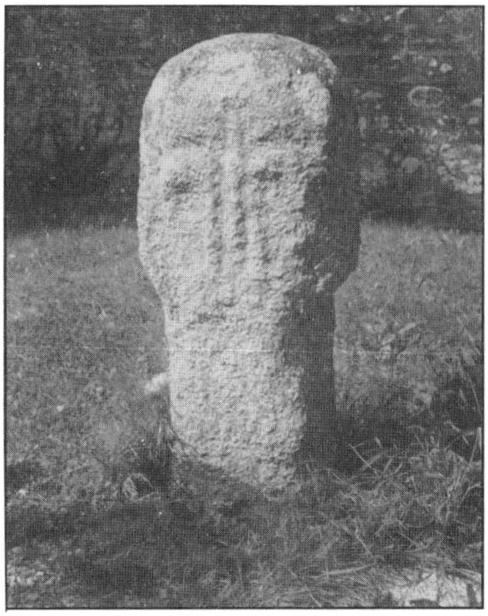

SX 0008, 7197 - Left hand side of south porch, Egloshayle Church. Access - Unlimited.

This second cross in the churchyard at Egloshayle reveals some curious markings in place of a cross symbol. Maclean suggested it was a fleur-de-lys, Blight agreed but Langdon was of the opinion it was only a cross with a wide vertical limb. It is difficult to decide who is correct as viewing the stone in different light and times of day gives a different impression.

Both this cross and Egloshayle No. 1 (see No. 29 in this guide) are sometimes referred to as 'Peverall's Cross' and have been linked with the ancient family of Peverall who owned the manor of Park through the medieval period. The author suggests that the family may have been responsible for their erection. Another cross in the parish of Blisland is also known as Peverall's Cross and may also be connected with the family.

Height 3' 2" (0.965M), Width of head 1' 3" (0.381M), Width of shaft 11" (0.28M), Thickness 8 1/2" (0.216M).

31

The Prior's Cross
Egloshayle

WHEEL HEADED WAYSIDE OR BOUNDARY CROSS

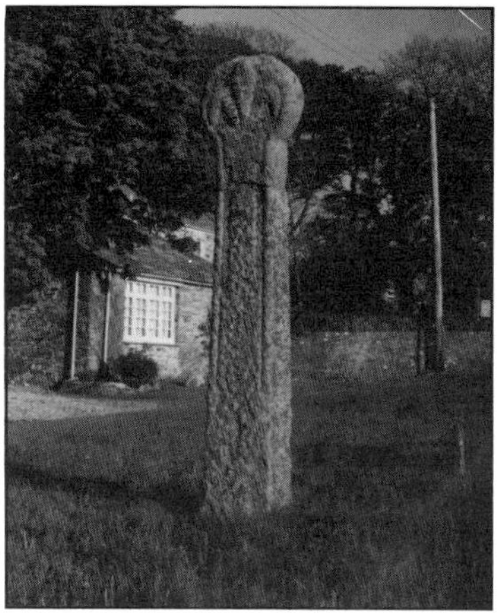

SX 0376, 6976 - In the village of Washaway on the A389 Wadebridge to Bodmin road, 4 miles from Wadebridge. Access - Unlimited.

The monument which is known as the Prior's Cross reveals a fleur-de-lys symbol, an emblem said by Maclean to be connected with Bodmin Priory. Again it has been suggested that the stone was found at Dunmere Woods.

In the 1890s only the cross head existed and the stone stood against the garden wall at the Washaway Inn; the property ceased to be an Inn many years ago. The fleur-de-lys symbol appears on both faces and is enclosed by a bead, which is extended down the modern shaft. The cross was re-erected in 1935 on a new shaft of ideal proportions by Sir Hugh Molesworth St. Aubyn of Pencarrow House and Mr. H.C. Babington of Croan.

Height 10' 7 1/2" (3.24M), Width of head 2' 3" (0.686M), Width of shaft (original) 1' 4" (0.406M), Width of new shaft 1' 4" to 1' 8" (0.406M to 0.509M), Thickness 9" (0.228M).

32

The Three Hole Cross
Egloshayle

HOLED WAYSIDE CROSS

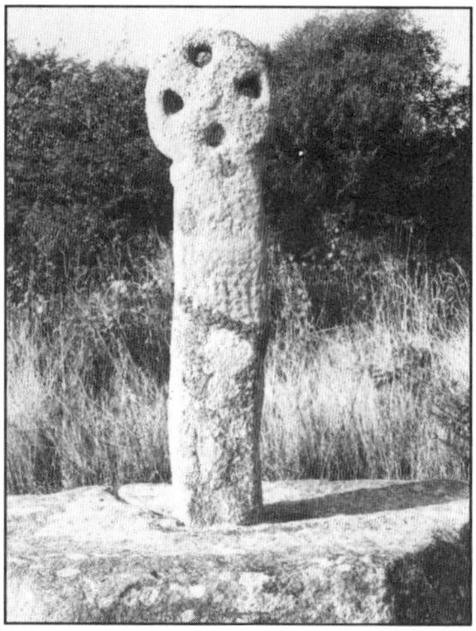

SX 0119, 7367 - 1 1/2 miles north-east of Wadebridge. At the intersection of six ancient roads; the main highway from Wadebridge to Camelford A39, a road from Chapel Amble to Pencarrow and a track from the Domesday Manor of Burniere to the Hill Fort of Castle Killibury and on to St. Mabyn. Access - Unlimited.

This quaint old stone was illustrated by Maclean as leaning out from the top of the hedge, but later in 1871 when he saw it again, it had been thrown down and fractured. Originally the cross stood diagonally opposite its present site on the south side of the highway. It was through the efforts of the churchwarden, Mr. Edward Pollard of Court Place, that the stone was preserved in a recess in the hedge. The stone remained built into the hedge until 1937 when due to road improvements it was taken down. It lay on the new wastrel created by the road alterations until it was re-erected in 1939. The restoration was carried out by the Wadebridge Old Cornwall Society, a base was provided by the De-Lank Quarries and the monument was re-dedicated by the Bishop of Truro on the 5th October 1939.

The stone and the area both take their name from the fact that the cross only has three holes; there is a central boss on the head of the stone, with a fourth hole started but not completed. The holes are positioned to display a St. Andrew's Cross. This is one of only two such stones in the county, the other being the St. Piran's Cross on Penhale Sands in the parish of Perranzabuloe. (See Mid Cornwall No. 76).

Height 5' 8" (1.73M), Width of head 1' 7 1/2" (0.495M), Width of shaft 11" (0.28M), Thickness 9" (0.230M)

33

Pencarrow Cross
Egloshayle
FOUR HOLED BOUNDARY CROSS

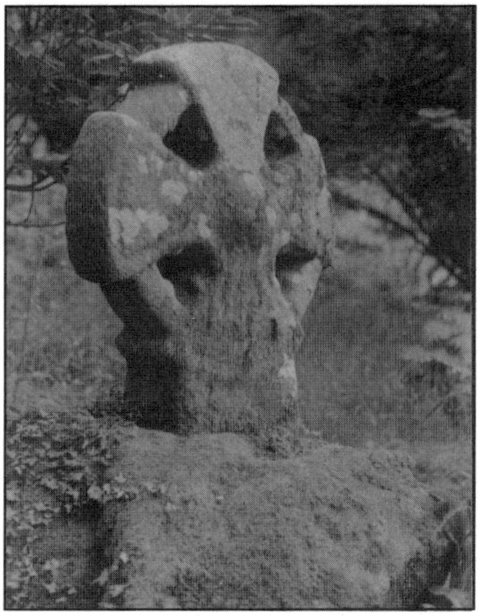

SX 0407, 7092 - Beside a garden path on the south-east side of Pencarrow House, Pencarrow Estate, Washaway, Bodmin. Access - Only available when the gardens are open to the public. For details of prices and times please see notice board at the entrance to the estate. (There is no free admission to view the cross only).

This large elegant cross head stands in the private grounds of Pencarrow House, the home of the Molesworth St. Aubyn family.

The cross head was found in about 1870, built into the hedge of the old deer park on the estate. It is supposed to have marked the original boundary of the Peverells estate of Park, of which Pencarrow was once a part. It was later removed into the gardens and erected on a large rock. The four holed cross head displays an equal limbed cross enclosed by an outer ring. The four holes are trefoil in shape and are formed by cusps on each limb and the ring, with a central boss in the middle. Langdon recorded that a cross shaft existed on the adjoining farm of Trescowe but this has unfortunately been lost.

Height 3' 7 1/ 2" (1.105M), Width of head 2' 11" (0.89M), Width of shaft 1' 4 1/2" (0.42M), Thickness 5" to 10" (0.127M to 0.255M).

34

Trelights Cross Base
St. Endellion
BASE OF WAYSIDE CROSS

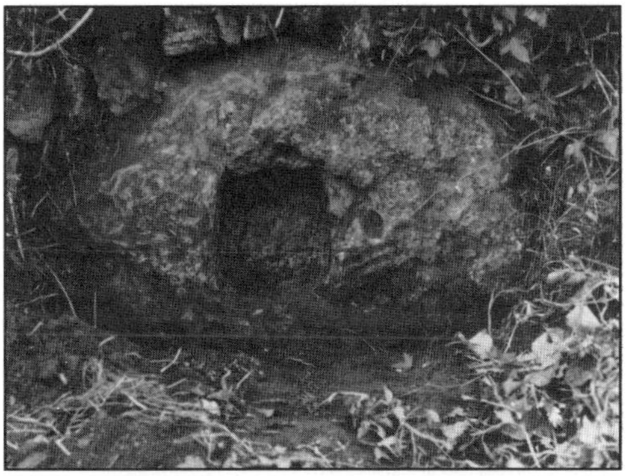

SW 9902, 7876 - 60 yards west, along the B3314 road from St Endellion church at a junction with a lane leading to Trelights village. Access - Unlimited.

This cross base was discovered set into the foot of the hedge on the western side of the lane, close to its junction with the main highway. The author was shown this previously unrecorded stone by Mr George Cowling, the late President of the Wadebridge Old Cornwall Society. A search by the author for the cross which the base supported has so far proved unsuccessful. The oval base stone is cut from a piece of greenstone - not granite - and displays a mortice. The author and members of the Old Cornwall Society have recently shifted the stone around the corner of the junction to a new site. Here the stone has been raised up so that its complete area can be seen.

Length 3' 11" (1.2M), Width 2' 5" (0.74M), Thickness Unknown, Mortice 10" by 12 1/2" (0.25M by 0.32M), Mortice depth 8" (0.2M).

35

Longcross
St. Endellion
INSCRIBED MEMORIAL CROSS

SW 9898, 7972 - 1 mile north-west of St. Endellion church, along a minor road leading from the east end of the churchyard. Access - Unlimited;

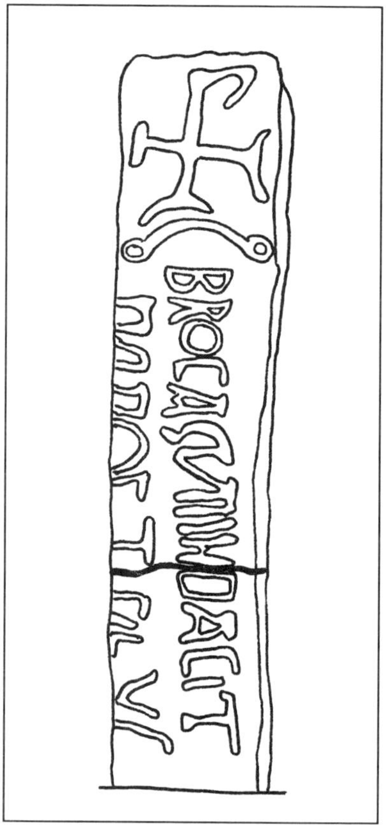

This stone may have once been connected with the ancient manor of Roscarrock, which lies to the north-west. It is the oldest and rarest early Christian monument in North Cornwall. The stone shows one of the earliest known Christian symbols on a stone monument, this is the Chi Rho monogram. The monogram is of an advanced style and displays a hooked P and a single transverse bar rather than the X symbol. The stone also bears an inscription to a person called Brocagnus in both Latin and Ogham script. It reads: *"BROCAGNI IHC IACIT NADOTTI FILIVS"*, which when translated is "BROCAGNI LIES HERE THE SON OF NADOTTI". It has been suggested that a similar inscription carved in Ogham once existed, although today there is no evidence to support this. On the reverse or northern face of the stone is an equal limbed cross carved in relief near the top of the shaft, with no further inscriptions or ornamentation evident.

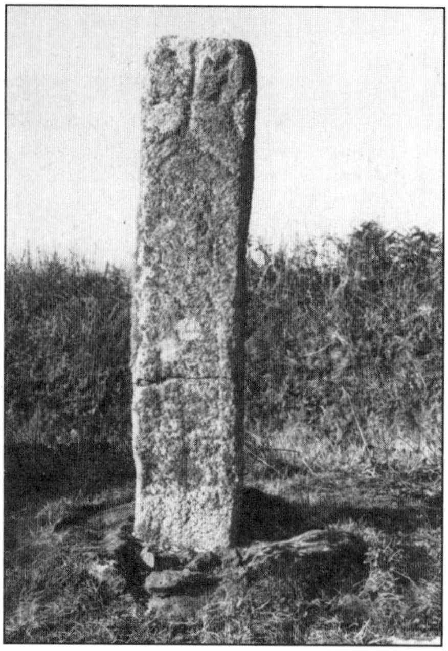

It has also been suggested that a small mortice or socket in the top of the pillar once supported a later additional cross head. Again this is only conjecture and cannot be substantiated as it could have been cut during its former use as a gatepost. In the history of Port Isaac and Port Quin by Dr. F. Trevan (1834), he mentions the Longcross, calling it "Higher Town Gate Cross", and records it under Roscarrock. At this time the shaft had already been thrown down and fractured according to Trevan.

During the last century the monument was removed to Doyden Headland (NGR SW 9775, 8060) by Mr. Symons of Gonvena where it suffered badly from erosion. Here the monument stood until 1932 when, thanks to the efforts of the Bodmin Old Cornwall Society, the stone was rescued and returned to its base stone which had remained *in situ* at Longcross.

Height 4' 11" (1.5M), Width of shaft 1' (0.3M), Thickness 8" (0.2M).

36

Tresungers Cross
St. Endellion
SEMI-GOTHIC LATIN CROSS

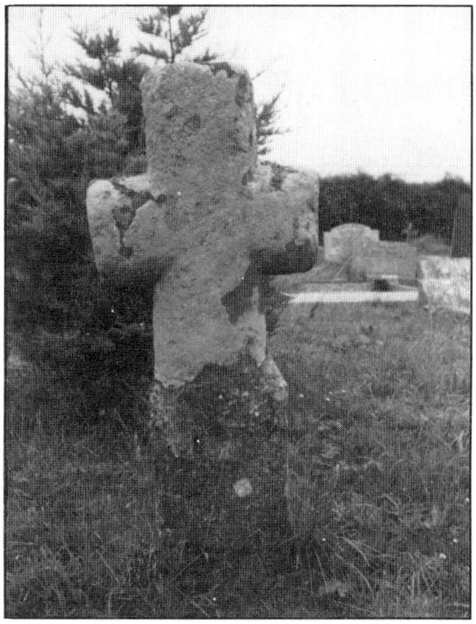

SW 9968, 7865 - Western side of extension to St Endellion churchyard. Access - Unlimited.

This Latin cross was first recorded in 1873 when it stood in a field on the Barton of Tresunger. It was later set up in front of the castellated manor house and eventually moved in 1922 to the churchyard. The size of this small cross gives the impression that it was possibly a gable cross, as there is no evidence that any additional shaft existed. The author considers that it was far too small to have been a free standing monument and he suggests that it may have been supported by an additional shaft when it stood in the field. Today the monument is cemented to a rough piece of stone to increase its height. The granite cross is circular in section - not octagonal - and is of late Gothic date. Its upper limb is slightly taller than the horizontal limbs.

Height 2' 2" (0.66M), Width of head 1' 5" (0.43M), Width of limbs and shaft 8" (0.2M).

37

Penally Terrace Cross
Forrabury
CROSS SLAB/PILLAR

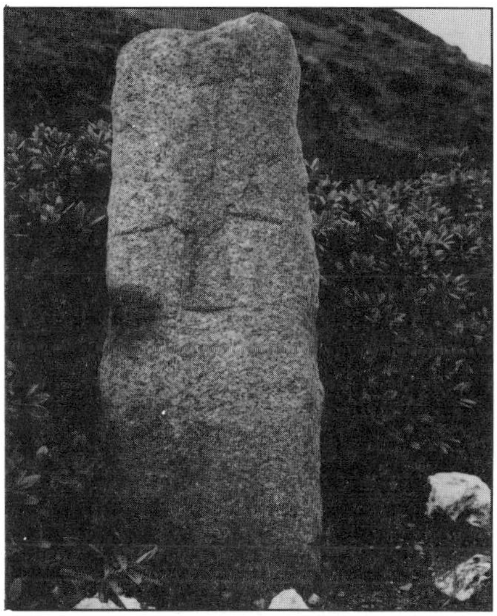

SX 0988, 9130 - This old stone stands in a flower border near Penally Terrace, a row of cottages on the north side of Boscastle harbour. The cottages are reached by the coastal footpath. Access - Although it stands on private ground it can easily be viewed from the adjacent public footpath.

The history of the stone is vague and two suggestions have been noted; one that the monument was discovered in the harbour and removed to the cliff top, and the other that the pillar is modern and cut by a local man. This roughly hewn granite stone displays a Greek type cross in relief on one side only, the reverse side is unworked. It has been included in this work due to its ancient appearance.

Height 3' 2" (0.965M), Width of shaft (top) 1' (0.3M), Width of shaft (bottom) 1' 2" (0.36M), Thickness 8" (0.2M), Raised cross height 1' 2" (0.36M), Raised cross width 11" (0.28M)

38

Church Path, Forrabury
Forrabury
WHEEL HEADED WAYSIDE CROSS

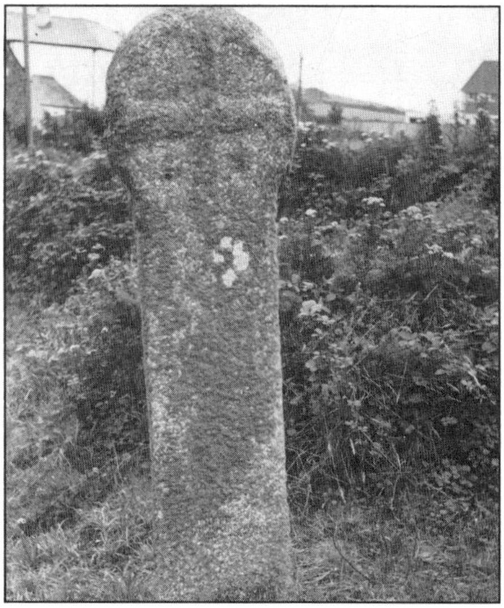

SX 0956, 9085 - On a footpath leading to Forrabury church only a few yards south of the churchyard. Access - Unlimited.

Immediately on walking up towards the church we will see the Forrabury Cross, standing beside a church path, only yards from the churchyard gate. Maclean recorded that it had been removed from another site, possibly a field close by known as Cross Park and marked No. 74 on the Tithe Apportionment Map. In the past it has evidently been used as a gatepost many times, as three holes in the monument show. The cross displays Greek type crosses on both faces but they have been badly eroded by the elements.

Height 5' 7" (1.7M), Width of shaft 1' 2" (0.36M), Width of head 1' 6" (0.46M), Thickness 8" (0.2M).

39

Lancarffe Cross
Helland
LANTERN CROSS

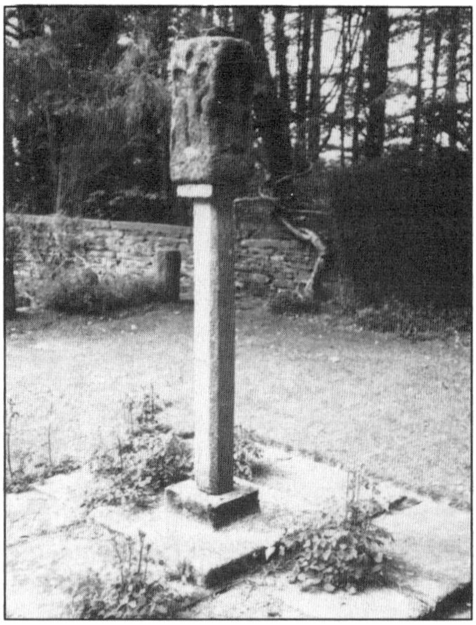

SX 0829, 6897 - In the grounds of Lancarffe House, 1 1/2 miles north-east of Bodmin. Access - The cross stands on private property, there is no public access except for when the gardens are open to the public once or twice a year.

Lancarffe was originally owned by the Bodmin Priory, which gives some reason for this elaborate monument to be found here. In 1850 the property was owned by the Hext family and the cross was removed to another of their family houses at Tredethy. Here it was seen by both Maclean and Langdon to be supported by a short octagonal base stone. In 1946 it was again brought back to Lancarffe and set up on a new slender shaft and stepped base. The old base stone still stands near a barn in the grounds of the property.

The cross displays the Crucifixion scene on the east side, with the Virgin Mary and Child depicted on the west side. The two remaining sides show single figures. The stone was originally recorded under the ecclesiastical parish of Bodmin, but today Lancarffe is situated in the parish of Helland, due to boundary changes.

Height of cross head 1' 10" (0.56M), Width 10" (0.255M), Total height on modern shaft 7' 6" (2.285M).

40

Anderton Mill Cross
St. Juliot
WHEEL HEADED BOUNDARY CROSS

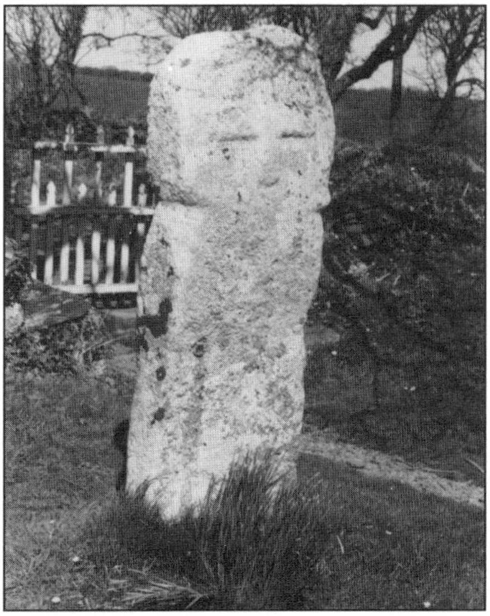

SX 1290, 9125 - St. Juliot church is situated 3/4 mile north of St. Michael's, Lesnewth. This cross stands on the northern side of the churchyard. Access - Unlimited.

Anderton Mill stands on the north bank of the river Valency which forms the boundary between St. Juliot and Lesnewth parishes. This crude example of a wheel type cross was actually found on the Lesnewth side, or south side of the valley, in use as a gatepost. The author suggests that the stone was probably a parish bound stone. There is still evidence of its former use as a gatepost with leaded holes for gate hangings still visible on its shaft. The cross was removed from beside the mill in 1852 and set up in the churchyard for preservation. On each face is displayed a Latin cross in relief with a bead running around the top of the head.

Height 5' 6" (1.68M), Width of head 2' (0.61M), Width of shaft 1' 10" to 2' (0.56M to 0.61M), Thickness 7 1/2" (0.19M).

41

St. Juliot's Cross
St. Juliot
WHEEL HEADED WAYSIDE CROSS

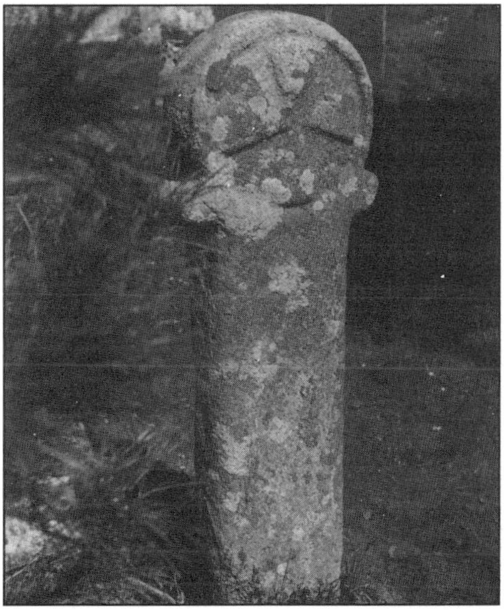

SX 1298, 9124 - Situated by the south-western entrance to the churchyard. Access - Unlimited.

This is one of the best preserved and executed crosses of its type in the county. Langdon considered it to be *in situ,* standing beside a churchyard stile. It marks a path leading from the churchyard through the Valency Valley to Boscastle.

The monument is almost perfect. Within a narrow bead around the head is displayed an equal limbed cross in high relief, the limbs made from four triangular sinkings. At the neck are projections of equal length and size. The reverse face is similar in style. In the author's view the wayside cross is of a very late date and perhaps even re-cut.

Height 6' 4 1/2" (1.94M), Width of head 1' 8 1/2" (0.52M), Width of shaft 1' 3 1/2" (0.39M), Width of projections 2' (0.61M), Thickness 6" to 9" (0.15M to 0.23M), Base stone 3' 3" x 2' 4" x 5 1/2" (1M x 0.71M x 0.14M).

42

Tregatheral Cross
St. Juliot

WHEEL HEADED WAYSIDE OR BOUNDARY CROSS

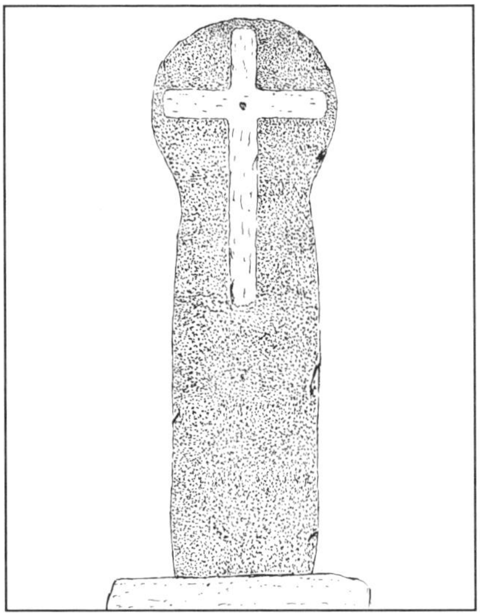

SX 1291, 9122 -Situated on the eastern side of St. Juliot churchyard. Access - Unlimited.

The third cross at St. Juliot is know as the Tregatheral Cross and was only set up in the churchyard in January 1953. It was found in the previous year in use as a gatepost, with its head buried downwards in the ground at an old mill on Tregatheral Farm, Minster. The monument was purchased by Mr. Biddick, a churchwarden at St. Juliot, from the farmer, Mr. Seldon of Tregatheral, and was removed to the churchyard for preservation. The fields of Tregatheral form part of the boundary between Minster and Lesnewth and the cross may have stood on this boundary known as Grylls Lane.

The cross is different in design from the two previous examples, having a Latin cross carved in relief on each side of the monument.

Height 4' 10" (1.47M), Width of head 1' 8" (0.51M), Width of shaft 1' 3" (0.38M), Thickness 8" (0.2M)

43

Polrode Cross
St. Kew

WHEEL HEADED WAYSIDE CROSS

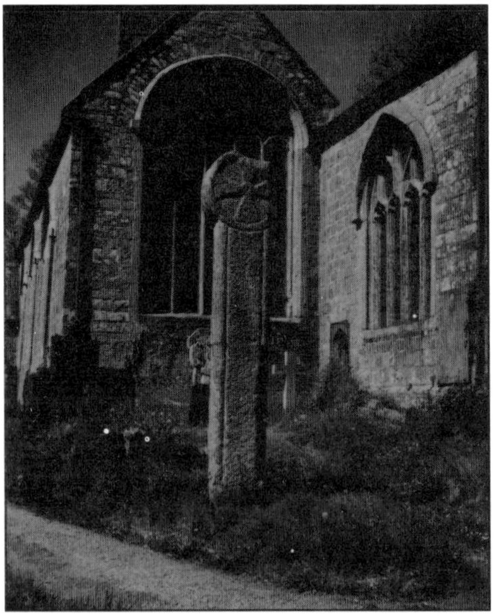

SX 0217, 7688 - South-east side of St. Kew churchyard. St. Kew churchtown is situated 4 miles north-east of Wadebridge, off the A39 highway to Camelford. Access - Unlimited.

The top section of this monument was found at Polrode Mill, in the beautiful Allen Valley. Here it was discovered in use as part of a footbridge across a stream leading to the mill. The head of the stone was cut off in line with the shaft so that it would fit closely to the next piece of granite in the bridge. In 1908, through the efforts of Mr. Nicholas Bray and Major Braddon of St. Kew, the stone was erected in the churchyard on a stepped base stone. Many years later the lower section of the cross was discovered by Mr. Bray at Higher Polrode Farm, in use as a jamb of the kitchen fireplace. In 1926, this section was also removed to the churchyard and both portions were reunited as a complete monument.

Height 9' 8" (2.946M), Height of top section 5' 5" (1.65M), Width of head 1' 10" (0.558M), Original width of head 2' 2" (0.66M), Width of shaft 1' 6" (0.46M), Thickness 9" (0.23M).

44

Skisdon Cross
St. Kew
LANTERN CROSS

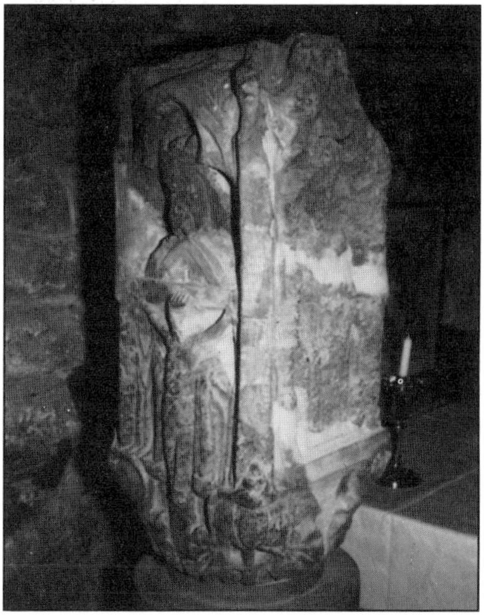

SX 0216, 7689 - Inside St. Kew parish church near to the font. Access - When the church is unlocked, normally open during daylight hours.

This Gothic lantern cross is one of two discovered in the parish of St. Kew, the second now stands in the churchyard at St. Neot and formerly came from Trewane in the north of the parish. This sculptured stone, like the Trewane Cross, was cut from Cataclewse stone - sometimes referred to as blue elvan stone - which came from the local St. Merryn quarries.

The large portion of the monument was found by the Rev. Dalton Jackson in the mud of the stream that runs through Skisdon gardens. The remaining fragments of the stone were discovered earlier in the boundary hedge of the Glebe. These parts of the cross were discovered between 1919 and 1924 and the monument was eventually restored. The lantern cross is carved on all four faces and depicts the Crucifixion scene, the Virgin Mary and Child and two single figures, either saints or bishops.

Height 2' 2" (0.66M), Width 1' (0.305M), Thickness 10 1/2" (0.266M)

45

Cross Shaft in Parish Church
St. Kew
SEMI-GOTHIC CROSS SHAFT

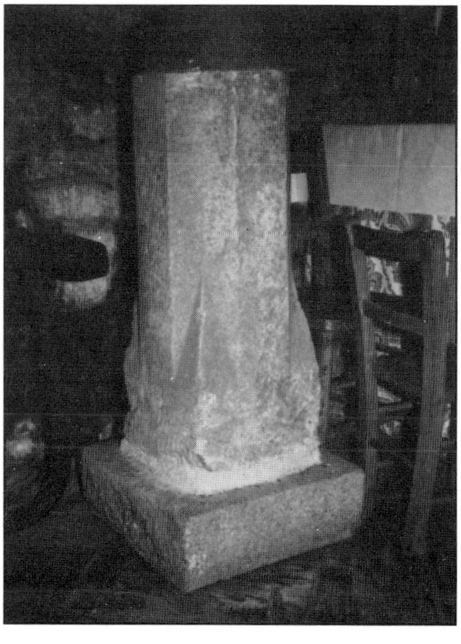

SX 0216, 7689 - This stone is also situated in the parish church and supports the lantern Cross (No. 44) previously mentioned. Access - When the church is unlocked, normally during daylight hours.

The lantern Cross (No. 44 in this guide) and the cross shaft are cut from two different types of stone and are therefore considered by the author to be originally two quite separate monuments.

The octagonal chamfered shaft is tapered and has stop chamfered angles at its base, a feature usually displayed on semi-Gothic type cross shafts. It would be a suitable shaft to support either a late Latin or lantern style cross head.

Height 2' 7" (0.79M), Width (approx.) 1' 0 1/2" (0.32M).

46

Cross Shaft in Tower
St. Kew
POSSIBLE CHURCHYARD CROSS

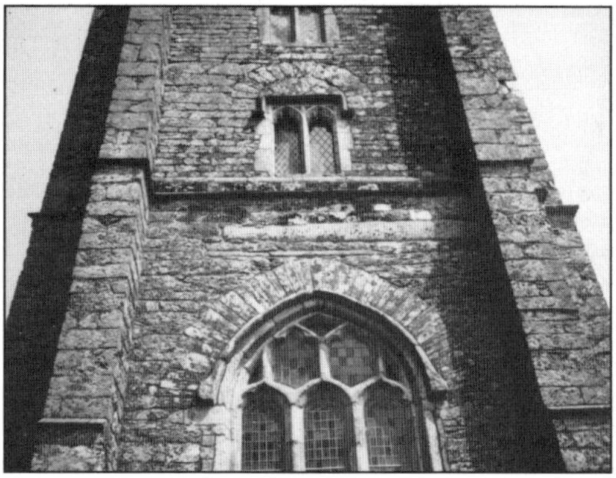

SX 0216, 7689 - West side of church tower above the window. Access - Unlimited.

In 1915 Stephens suggested that a large length of granite built horizontally into the external wall of the church tower, may be the original churchyard cross. The tower is built almost entirely from slate stone except for this granite shaft. Stephens also went on to suggest that the left-hand side of the stone was the tenon of the monument. Unfortunately without a much closer examination it will be difficult to prove conclusively whether this length of granite is an ancient monument or simply a building stone.

Length (approx.) 11' 6" (3.5M), Width 1' (0.3M).

47

Chapel Amble Cross
St. Kew
WHEEL HEAD WAYSIDE CROSS

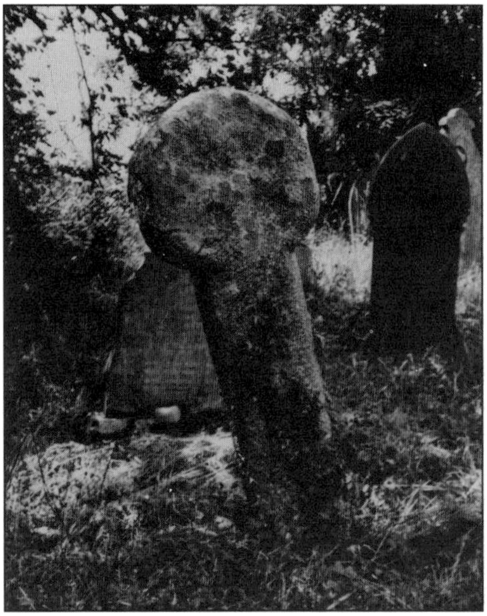

SX 0215, 7691 - North side of St. Kew churchyard, among the tombstones, and close to the western boundary wall. Access - Unlimited.

This cross was discovered in use as a gatepost at Chapel Amble in 1912 and was removed by Mr. Cleave to the churchyard, where it was placed over a family grave. The cross is a well executed monument, the head displays a cross with widely expanded limbs and is almost Maltese in style, and a faint bead also exists. Its shaft is unusual, having chamfered sides, suggesting it to be a late example of a wheel type cross. The stone was found close to the site of the ancient chapel of St. Aldhelm, of which no remains exist, and was probably an old guide post to the site.

Height 5' 2" (1.58M), Width of head 1' 11" (0.58M), Width of shaft 1' 3" (0.38M), Thickness 9 1/2" (0.24M).

48

Trequite Cross
St. Kew
WHEEL HEADED WAYSIDE OR BOUNDARY CROSS

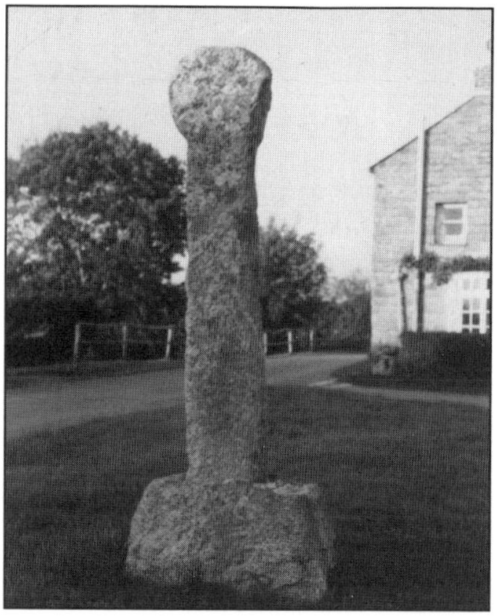

SX 0294, 7694 - The village of Trequite lies half a mile due east of St. Kew churchtown. The monument stands on the village green. Access - Unlimited.

This is one of two crosses which have been discovered in Trequite village. In 1913 the Rev. Dalton Jackson discovered this cross head built as part of the threshold of a doorway to a cow shed at Trequite Farm. The stone remained at the farm, where Ellis viewed it in 1938 and discovered the lower section of the monument built into an adjacent doorway. The two pieces were joined, mounted on a new base and re-erected by the Wadebridge Old Cornwall Society on the green in 1947. The cross was dedicated by the Bishop of Truro, Dr. J.W. Hunkin with the Rev. A. Longden, Rector of St. Breock, assisting.

Height (complete) 7' 4 1/2" (2.25M), Width of head 1' 4" (0.4M), Width of shaft 11" to 1'2" (0.28M to 0.35M), Length of upper section of shaft 2' 2" (0.66M), Thickness 7" to 10" (0.18M to 0.25M)

49

Trequite Cross Head Fragment
St. Kew
WHEEL HEADED WAYSIDE OR BOUNDARY CROSS

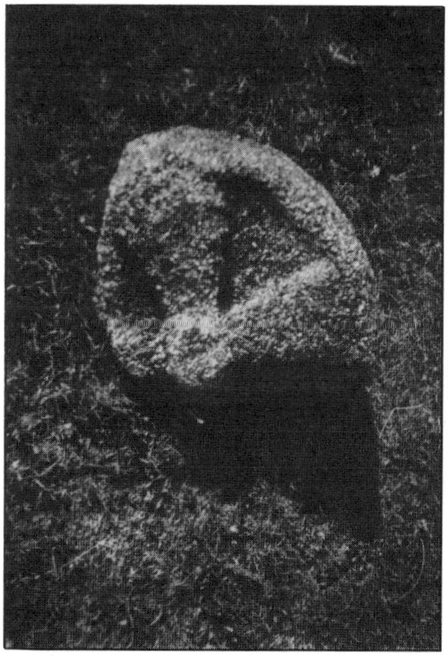

SX 0339, 7566 - In a cottage garden at St. Kew Highway. Access - There is no public access, the stone is on private property.

This second cross head was found at Trequite, but is only a fragment. It was also found in 1913 by Mr. James Pinch of St. Kew, built into a hedge of a cottage garden close to the village. Ellis suggested that the stone was originally a boundary stone which marked the extent of the Glebe. The stone was later removed to the garden of Mr. Nicholas Bray, the St. Kew historian, and added to his collection of ancient stone relics. These were left in the care of the Wadebridge Old Cornwall Society at the time of his death.

Height 1' 4 1/2" by 1' (0.42M by 0.3M), Thickness 6" (0.15M).

50

Jobs Cross
St. Kew

WHEEL HEADED WAYSIDE CROSS

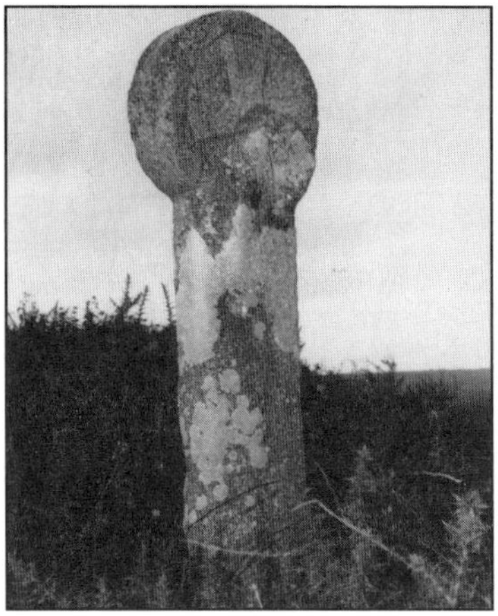

SX 0116, 7671 - The cross stands on a staggered crossroads, half a mile west of St. Kew churchtown on the road to Chapel Amble, which is dissected by a road leading to St. Endellion. Access - Unlimited.

Again, the discovery of this monument was due to the interest and enthusiasm of Mr. Bray, who first noticed this cross in 1906. It was then serving as a gatepost beside an old path leading from Jobs Farm to Carclaze, a farm on the opposite bank of the river. Mr. Bray later had the cross removed to Jobs Tenement, where it remained for many years. The stone was in a very mutilated state, with two thirds of the cross head missing and gate hangings leaded into the shaft. After the Second World War the Wadebridge Old Cornwall Society was instrumental in having the old cross repaired. The stone was taken to De Lank Granite Quarry at St. Breward where the head was reconstructed skilfully by local stone masons. The restored cross was erected in 1952.

Height 6' 4" (1.93M), Width of head 1' 11" (0.59M), Width of shaft 1' 1" (0.33M), Thickness 7 1/2" (0.19M)

51

Churchyard Cross
Laneast

FOUR HOLED CHURCHYARD CROSS

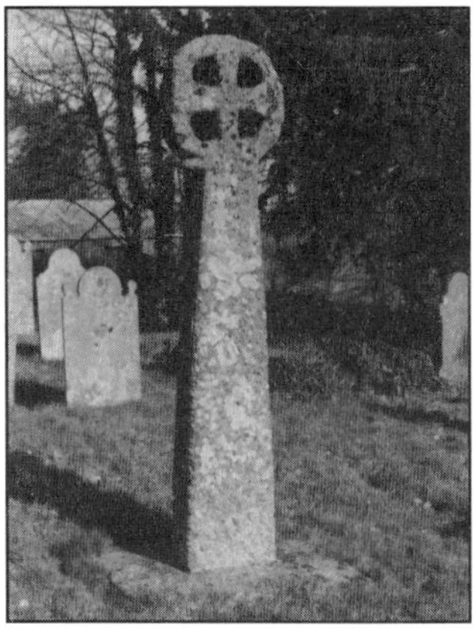

SX 2281,8397 - Laneast churchtown is situated 7 miles west of Launceston, 1/4 mile south of the A395 Davidstow to Launceston road. Access - Unlimited

The cross head and upper section of shaft on this monument is the only original remains of the churchyard cross. It was discovered in June 1952 by the parish sexton while digging a grave on the south side of the churchyard. It was found among discarded building material, three feet below ground level, which lead Ellis to suggest that the stone may have been dumped there at the time that the church was rebuilt in 1437.

Under the guidance of the Rev. E.J. Saunders, the vicar, the monument was retrieved and the local Old Cornwall Society informed at Launceston. The restoration work was carried out by the De Lank Granite Quarries and supervised by Launceston O.C.S. in 1954. A new shaft and base stone were cut and joined to the original shaft and the completed monument was set up opposite the south porch, close to where it was discovered. The stone cross was re-dedicated in June 1954 by the Assistant Bishop of Truro, the Rt. Rev. John Wellington and the Rev. Saunders.

The cross head itself is plain, with the expanded limbs of the cross slightly raised in relief above that of the enclosing ring. The most unusual architectural feature displayed on the cross is an abacus or collar-like bead at the neck of the monument. This characteristic is only seen on two other Cornish crosses; in the churchyard of Michaelstow and in Lawhitton church. Below this collar can be seen the remains of a bead running down the shaft and also signs of some incised decoration.

Height of head 3' 10" (1.18M), Width of head 1' 11" (0.585M), Width of shaft 11" (0.28M), Thickness 8" (0.2M), Total Height 8' 4" (2.54M).

52

Laneast Downs Cross
Laneast
WHEEL HEADED WAYSIDE CROSS

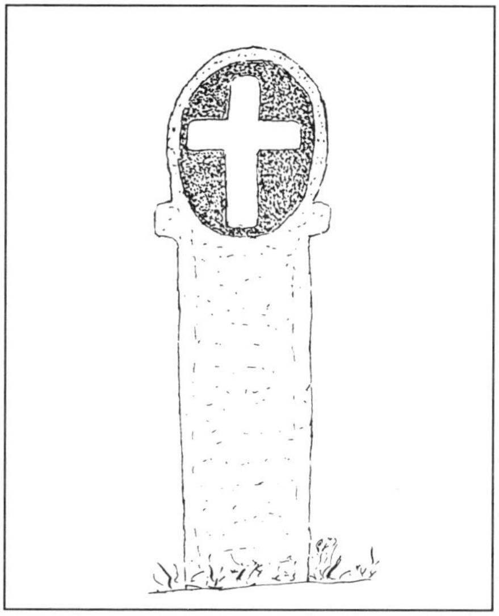

SX 2350,8551 - 3/4 mile north of the A395 road from Davidstow to Launceston, near High Hall Farm on Laneast Downs. Access - Unlimited.

Historians consider this cross to be *in situ*, marking a track towards the parish church, although no evidence of a base stone exists today. The cross also marks a route diagonally across the Downs via High Hall and Badgall to Tresmeer churchtown. The stone commands a magnificent view towards the north coast and is surprisingly well preserved considering its exposed position. The cross head is elliptical in shape rather than round, and displays a Latin cross in relief, with the recessed area enclosed in a bead. The reverse face is similar in style. The monument has projections at the neck, a characteristic seen on many of the north Cornwall crosses, and is unusual in that it is cut from Polyphant stone rather than granite.

Height 6' 5" (1.955M), Length of head 2' 3" (0.685M), Width of head 1' 11" (0.585M), Width of shaft 1' 8 1/2" (0.52M), Thickness 8" (0.2M).

53

Tregoodwell Cross
Lanteglos by Camelford
WHEEL HEADED WAYSIDE CROSS

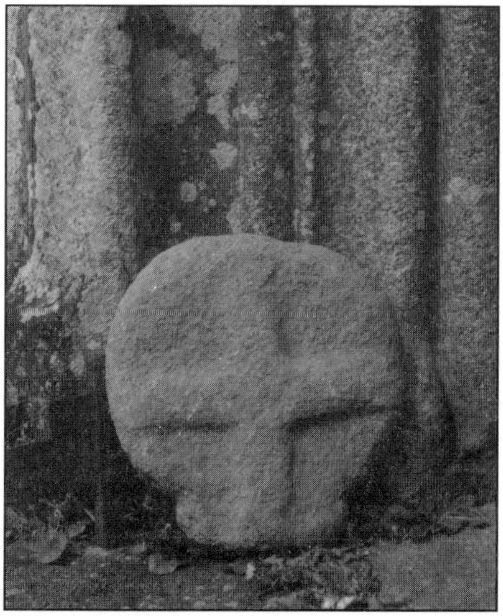

SX 0881, 8234 - This cross head sits beside the font inside the parish church. The church lies remote from the town of Camelford, being in a valley 1 1/2 miles to the south-west. Access - In recent years the church has been kept locked during the day but a key can be obtained from a nearby cottage (for address see the Church notice board).

This cross head was originally found with a small portion of shaft in June 1891, while part of a hedge was being dismantled to form a new gateway at Tregoodwell. Here it was set up on an old Camelford boundary stone, near the junction of two lanes leading to the A39 road. The higher lane is known as Higher Cross Lane.

The cross may have formerly marked the ancient track across the moor to Tyland Corner on Davidstow Moor. The monument was later removed to Lanteglos church for preservation early in the 20th century.

Height 1' 5" (0.43M), Width of head 1' 3" (0.38M), Width of shaft 8 1/2" (0.22M), Thickness 4" (0.1M)

54

Castle Goff Stone
Lanteglos by Camelford
INSCRIBED CROSS SHAFT

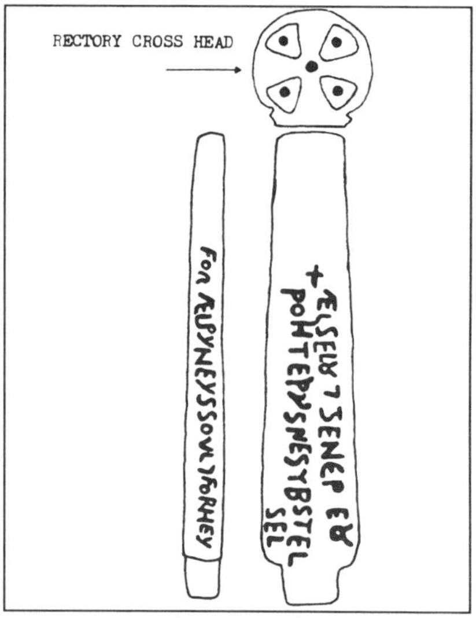

SX 0880, 8233 - This stone stands in the churchyard, close to the south aisle of the church. Access - Unlimited.

This stone is known as the Castle Goff (Castle Gough) Stone, and the small cross head close to it was once fixed to its top. The inscribed stone is of Saxon date and was first recorded in the 1870s, propping up the side wall of an old barn at Castle Goff Farm to the north-west of the churchyard.

Maclean noted that the stone was removed to the rectory garden by the Rev. Wilkinson in 1877. Here the cross head which was already in the garden, was mounted on its top (see No. 55 in this guide). The joint monument remained in the rectory gardens until the turn of the century, when it was again divided and both stones placed in the churchyard by the Rev. Robert Roe. The inscription on the shaft - in two vertical lines down the face and one line down the edge - reads: *"Aelselth 7 Genereth wohte thisne sybstel for Aelwines soul 7 for heysel"*. This translated reads: "Aelseth and Generath wrought this personal memorial for the soul of Aelwine and for themselves".

The most important feature illustrated by Langdon is unfortunately buried, this being a tenon cut on the lower end of the shaft. Inscribed stones did not normally have base stones, and the tenon suggests that it could be an inscribed cross shaft. A small drilling can also be seen on the top of the shaft, possibly for fixing the cross head.

Height 6' 7" (2M), Width of shaft (top) 1' 2" (0.35M), Width of shaft (bottom) 1' 7" (0.48M), Thickness 7" (0.18M)

55

Rectory Cross Head
Lanteglos by Camelford
WHEEL HEADED CROSS

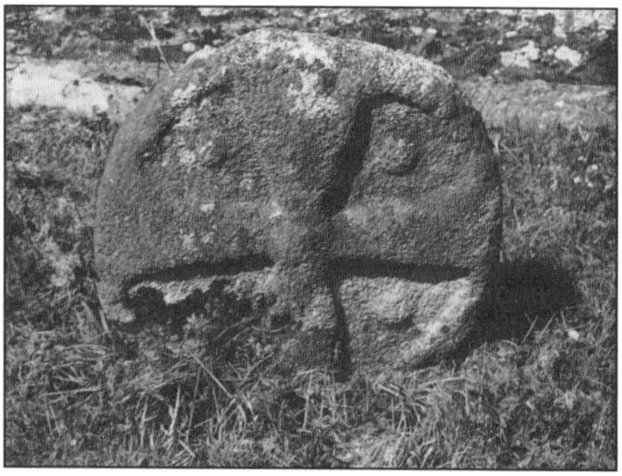

SX 0880, 8233- The cross head is situated a few yards to the east of the Castle Goff stone which formerly supported it, in Lanteglos churchyard. Access - Unlimited.

When first recorded this stone was standing on the rocky island of a fishpond at Lanteglos Rectory and was later erected on the Castle Goff stone. This stone is of special architectural interest, displaying five small bosses on an equal limbed cross. One boss is in the centre and another on each of the triangular sinkings between the limbs. There are similarities between this monument and the Trevena or Trevillet cross at Tintagel (see No. 97 in this guide) which also displays an inscription and bosses.

Height 2' (0.61M), Width of head 2' (0.61M), Thickness 10" (0.255M)

56

Valley Truckle Cross
Lanteglos by Camelford
WHEEL HEADED WAYSIDE CROSS

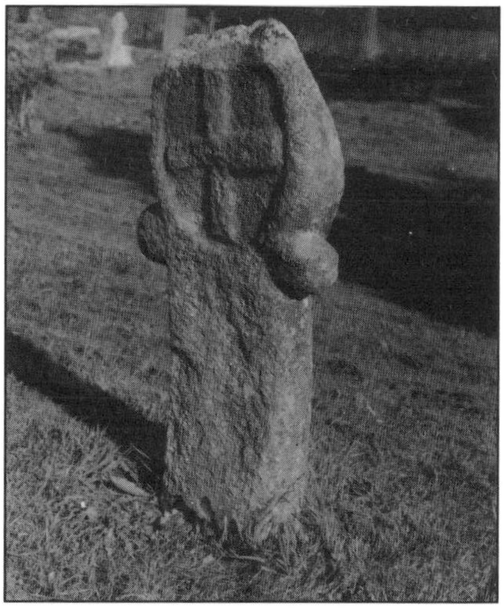

SX 0880, 8234 - Almost opposite the Castle Goff stone on the southern side of the churchyard path at Lanteglos by Camelford. Access - Unlimited.

This is the largest of the Camelford crosses and was discovered at a place called Valley Truckle, where the A39 trunk road is met by the B3266 Boscastle road and a minor road south-east to Advent parish. It was found set in the ground with its head downwards, near a blacksmith's shop, which formerly stood near the crossroads. It had been in this position for years and had been used for the binding of iron tires on cart wheels, for which purpose a part of the shaft had been rounded off. The huge wayside cross is in a good state of preservation, although the wide beading is damaged at the top of the head. The limbs are inclined to the right, which is not unusual for a wayside stone; many are rudely executed. Although projections at the neck of crosses are common in the Camelford and St. Clether area, this monument displays unusually large projections, almost like stunted arms. The monument leans backwards by 15 degrees.

Height 4' 11" (1.5M), Width of head 2' 8" (0.81M), Width of projections 2' 8" (0.81M), Thickness 5 1/2" (0.14M).

57

Trewalder Cross
Lanteglos by Camelford
WHEEL HEADED BOUNDARY OR WAYSIDE CROSS

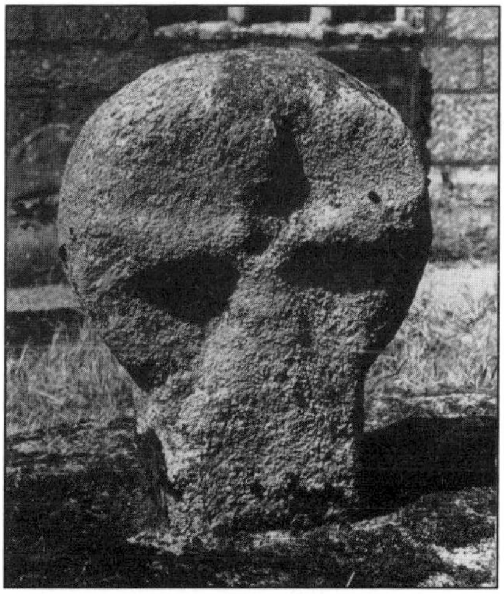

SX 0880, 8234 - In the churchyard, a few yards to the east of the Valley Truckle Cross. Access - Unlimited.

This small cross head was found at Trewalder, which is situated 1 1/2 miles west of Lanteglos Church and is known by that name. Maclean recorded that the cross formerly stood in the hedge at the corner of a field called Great Bovetown. It was later shifted to an opposite hedge when the road was widened. According to Ellis the stone was brought to the churchyard in 1912 for preservation and he also went on to state that he made a search for the base stone at Trewalder, which he was unable to find. The author has found this somewhat confusing as the Trewalder cross sits in a socket in the churchyard, identical in size to the one illustrated by Langdon and photographed by Ellis. Measurements by the author appear to conclude that the base is the original. The cross head has expanded limbs on either face, with a small hole or indentation in the centre.

Height 2' 4 1/2" (0.72M), Width of head 1' 8" (0.51M), Thickness 6" (0.15M), Base stone 4' by 3' 11" by 5" (1.22M by 1.19M by 0.12M).

58

Rectory Cross Lanteglos by Camelford

WHEEL HEADED WAYSIDE CROSS

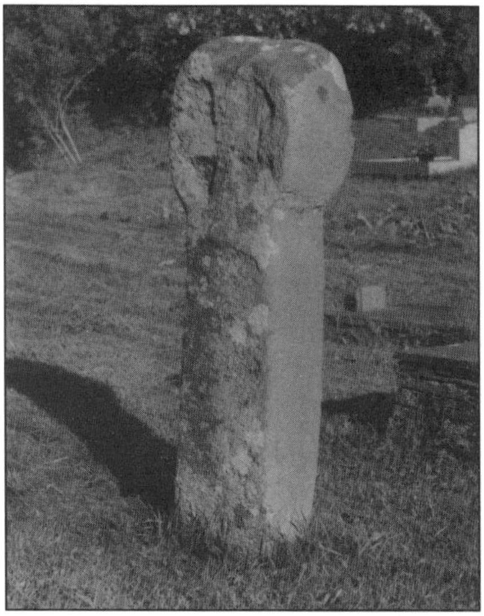

SX 0880, 8234 - In the churchyard, a few yards to the east of the Trewalder Cross. Access - Unlimited.

When first recorded by Blight in 1858, this cross had already been removed to the Rectory gardens. He stated that it was removed from the highway for preservation. The highway referred to would have probably been the A39 Wadebridge to Bude road.

The monument displays an entasis on only one side, this is a curvature of the shaft, the other side may have been erased when the cross was utilised as a gatepost prior to being rescued. The head has an equal limbed cross with expanded ends enclosed in a narrow bead, the cross on one face is slightly inclined to the right.

Height 5' 3 1/2" (1.61M), Width of head 1' 9" (0.53M), Width of shaft 1' 2" (0.36M), Thickness 9" (0.23M)

59

Trevia Walls Cross Lanteglos by Camelford

WHEEL HEADED WAYSIDE CROSS

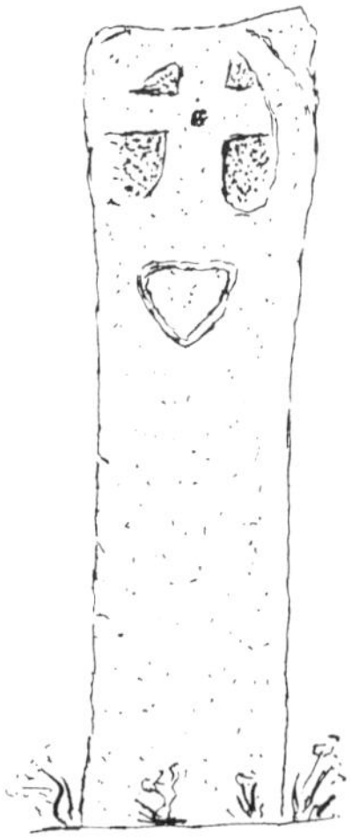

SX 0973, 8336 - 1 mile north-east of Lanteglos Church, at a road junction known as Trevia Walls, 1/4 mile north off the B3266 highway. Access - Unlimited.

When this cross was seen by Maclean in the 1870s, it was serving as a gatepost, and he hoped it would soon be moved from this ignominious position.

In 1984 the cross was damaged by farm machinery entering the field. This prompted its removal, but once repaired by St. Breward stonemasons at Hantergantick quarry it was returned and re-positioned close to its old site. At last Maclean's hope was fulfilled, although the Old Cornwall Society had discussed removing the stone to a nearby grass verge for additional safety. The monument is unusual, having an incised shield upon its shaft. The head displays a Latin cross in relief on both faces, although badly mutilated.

Height 5' 2" (1.58M), Width of head 1' 6 1/2" (0.47M), Width of shaft 1' 2" (0.36M), Thickness 8 1/2" (0.22M).

60

Trevia Cross
Lanteglos by Camelford
WHEEL HEADED WAYSIDE CROSS

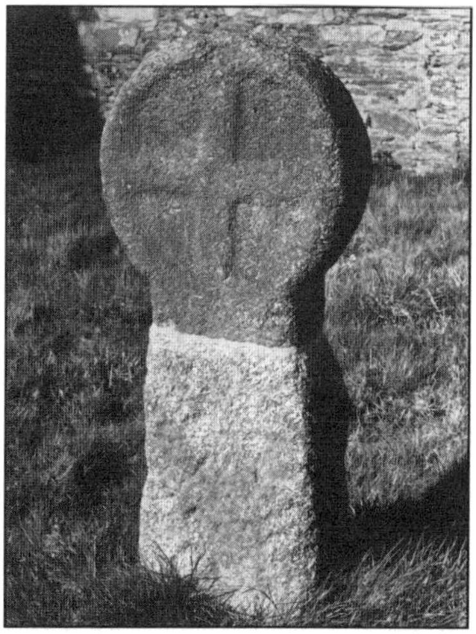

SX 1013, 8346 - At a crossroads, beside the B 3266 highway from Camelford towards Boscastle at a place known as Sportsmans. Access - Unlimited.

The stone was brought to the attention of Langdon by Mr J. R Collins of Bodmin, who stated that the granite cross was found in a hedge in August 1894, some 300 yards from the Camelford Workhouse. It was found by Mr. Nathaniel Stephens of Trevia Farm who placed it in his garden for safety. Here the stone stood until about 1970 when it was re-erected on a modern shaft, close to the crossroads. The monument displays an equal limbed cross within a narrow bead on either face.

Height of original stone 2' (0.61M), Height (overall) 4' 2" (1.27M), Width of head 1' 9" (0.53M), Width of shaft 1' 3" (0.33M), Thickness of cross 7" (0.18M).

61

Gothic Cross in Churchyard
St. Mary Magdalene
Launceston
LANTERN CROSS

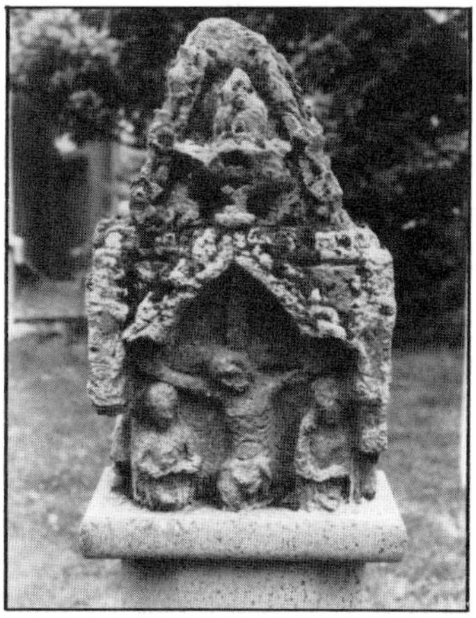

SX 3323, 8465 - On the eastern side of St. Mary Magdalene churchyard in Launceston. Access - Unlimited.

This skilfully carved lantern cross was first illustrated by Blight in 1858, mounted on the churchyard wall at St. Marys and was shown in a mutilated condition. Later it was renovated, with the addition of a decorative pyramid shaped top by Victorian craftsmen, and erected as a memorial stone on the grave of the Lawrence family. Here the cross head stood on a modern shaft until about the year 1958, when it was broken by a boy who tried to climb the monument. The cross was removed to the church crypt for storage until it was re-erected on a granite plinth by Launceston Old Cornwall Society in 1978, their Silver Jubilee Year.

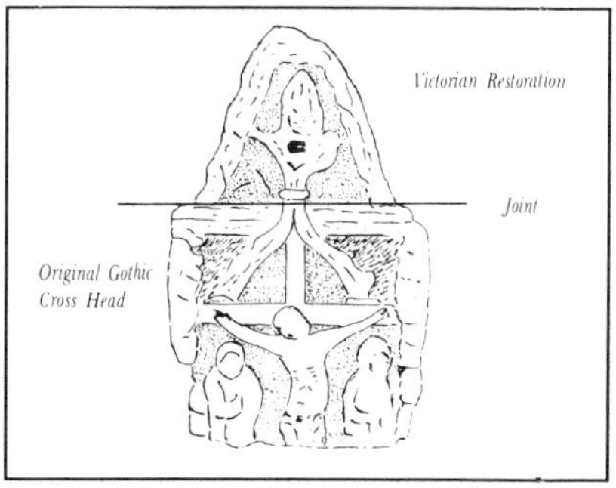

The cross head is carved from Cataclewse stone and depicts Christ on the Cross with two attendants, said to be his Mother and St. John.

On the reverse or north face are figures of the Virgin Mary and Child with an attendant on each side. The east face has a single figure of a woman and on the western face a man holding either a staff or a sword.

Height 1' 11" (0.585M), Width 1' 2" (0.355M), Thickness 8" (0.2M)

62

Cross Shaft in Churchyard St. Mary Magdalene Launceston

GOTHIC CROSS SHAFT

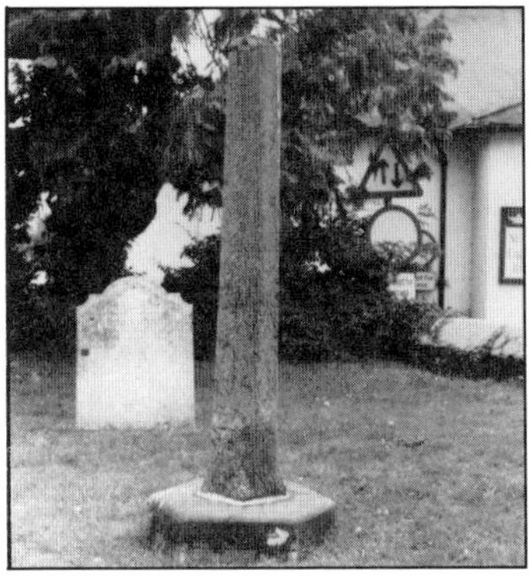

SX 3323, 8465 - On the eastern side of St. Mary Magdalene churchyard in Launceston, close to the Gothic cross head (No. 62). Access - Unlimited.

This Gothic cross shaft stands just a few feet to the south of the lantern cross head and is octagonal in section. The stone is cut from a piece of greenstone and displays chamfered stops near its base. The shaft has been fractured in the past, and a joint can be seen a foot from the base. The base stone is made up of two hexagonal blocks of stone. It is quite probable that this is the original cross shaft for the lantern cross (No. 61) as the two stones are of coeval dates and similar materials.

Height 6' (1.83M), Width of shaft (at top) 8" (0.2M), Width of shaft (at base) 10 1/2" (0.265M)

63

Dunheved Cross St. Mary Magdalene Launceston

GOTHIC CROSS

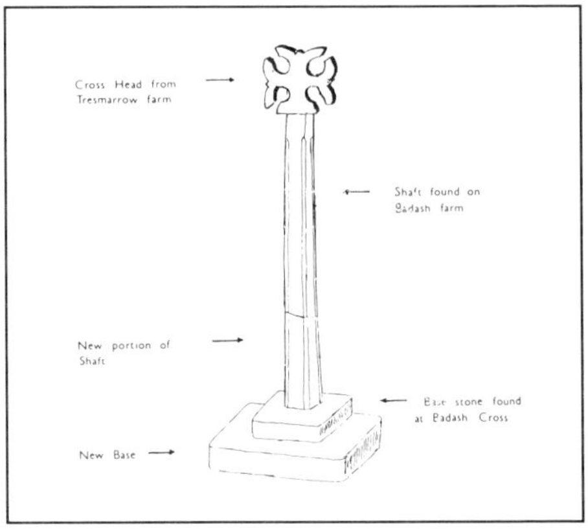

SX 3315, 8365 - At the end of a cul-de-sac off Landlake Road, overlooking the new Launceston by-pass. Access - Unlimited.

This impressive monument, now known as Dunheved Cross, was erected on Coronation Day the 27th June 1902, on the site known as Dunheved or Badash Cross. Langdon recorded that a cross head was discovered in a field near the site of the Alexander Slate Quarry at Tresmarrow Farm and was preserved at the Launceston Museum, he also noted that a cross base existed at Badash. At the beginning of the century Mr. C.F. Cowland, a member of Launceston Historical Society, discovered a large piece of octagonal cross shaft at Badash Farm. On comparing measurements of this shaft and the Badash cross base still built into a hedge, Mr. Cowland considered that if the shaft was complete it might fit the socket. Later, remembering the discovery of the cross at Tresmarrow, Mr. Cowland drew a scaled diagram of the three old fragments joined together as one monument. On seeing the diagram Mr. Coode, the owner of Badash, offered to finance the project. Two new pieces of stone were added to form the monument, a section of shaft and a lower base stone. The project was undertaken by the Launceston Historical Society which had the base stone inscribed: *"Dunheved Cross, this cross was restored and replaced near its original site on the Coronation of King Edward VII, 27th June 1902".*

In 1974 the monument was removed for preservation while the new Launceston by-pass was built, it was later replaced near its former site.

Cross head width 1' 6" (0.46M), Cross head height 1' 10" (0.56M), Cross head thickness 5" (0.128M), Badash shaft length 4' 8 1/2" (1.435M), Badash shaft width 6 1/2" to 10 1/2" (0.165M to 0.265M), New shaft length 2' 9 1/2" by 2' 10 1/2" by 6" (0.85M by 0.875M by 0.15M).

64

Cross Head at Southgate
St. Mary Magdalene
Launceston

SEMI - GOTHIC LATIN CROSS

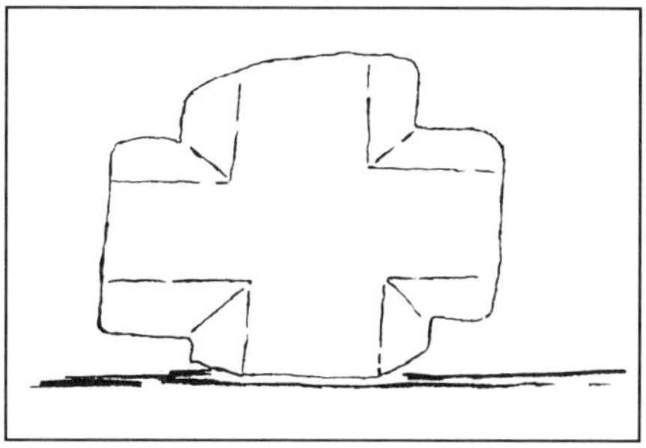

SX 3331, 8462 - Fixed to the wall at Launceston's South Gate. Access - Unlimited.

This semi-Gothic style cross head can be seen cemented to a wall along with other ecclesiastical stone fragments, probably removed at some time from the site of St. Thomas's Priory. When seen in 1954 by Mary Henderson, three small crosses stood on this wall but on returning in 1980 she could only locate one.

The stone appears to be the head of a Latin cross, it is octagonal in section and has remarkably short limbs. There are many missing crosses in and around Launceston; Pages Cross, Pennygillam and even the head of the Newport Cross (see No. 66 in this guide). This stone may be one of these. The author has been unable to trace any history concerning this cross or the two others which are known to have existed.

Height 1' 3" (0.38M), Width 1' 2" (0.355M), Thickness 5 1/2" (0.14M)

65

Newport Cross
St. Stephen by Launceston

MARKET CROSS

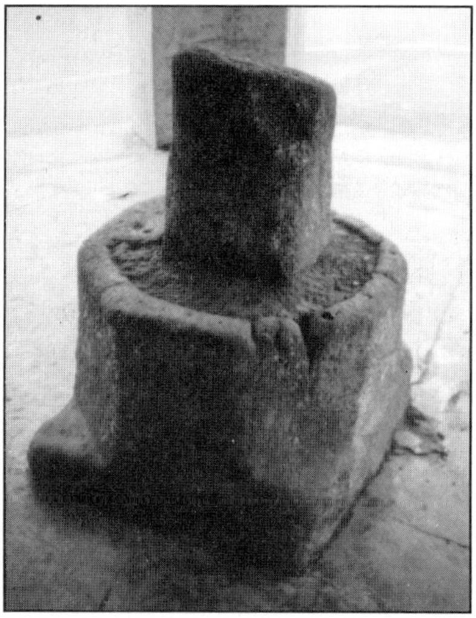

SX 3282, 8518 - Under a concrete shelter in the village of Newport between Launceston town and St. Stephen's church. Access - Unlimited.

This is one of the few examples of a market cross in Cornwall; in this case only the massive granite base stone and stump of the shaft exist today. In 1829 a concrete shelter was built over the monument by the Duke of Northumberland, who was hereditary Constable of the Castle and High Steward of Launceston. This octagonal structure has tall open arches on five of its sides and stands at the junction of the A388 Holsworthy road with the minor road leading up to St. Stephens.

The market cross in many English villages was the focal point of the village. Market stalls were set up around it, proclamations read out, punishments delivered and deals agreed; all at the cross. Newport was once an ancient borough and delivered two Members to Parliament and according to Ellis these Members of Parliament were proposed and seconded at the foot of the cross.

Many English villages have had similar structures built over their market crosses, and some have a canopied structure with a cross surmounting it, eg. Chichester and Malmesbury.

The medieval cross base is square at the bottom but octagonal at the top, due to its chamfered sides. The stump of the shaft, although very worn, is also octagonal in section.

Height of shaft 1' 8" (0.51M), Width of shaft 1' 1" (0.33M), Base stone 3' (0.915M) by 2' 8" (0.81M), Base stone height 2' (0.61M)

66

Cross in Churchyard
St. Thomas by Launceston
CROSS SLAB

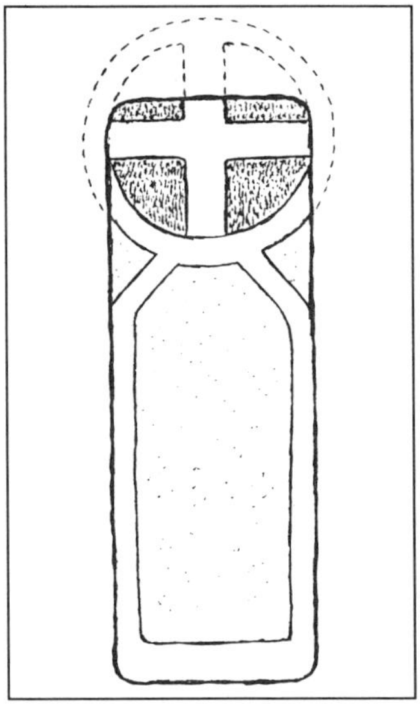

SX 3280, 8507 - St. Thomas churchyard lies close to the river Kensey, in the valley between Launceston town and St. Stephens. Access - Unlimited.

This slab of granite displays the remains of a wheel type cross on it and was discovered built into the chancel wall when the church was rebuilt between the years 1869 and 1870. The slab leans against a wall on the south-east side of the churchyard, close to where a path leads to the old priory site. The stone is unique in style, it is rectangular in shape, having been re-cut possibly for use as a building stone. This has caused the wheel of the cross and the upper limb to be destroyed. All that now remain are the horizontal and lower limbs in relief formed by triangular sinkings between the limbs.

Height 3' 6" (1.065M), Width 1' 3" (0.38M), Thickness 6" (0.15M)

67

Treniffle Cross
Lawhitton
FOUR HOLES CHURCHYARD CROSS

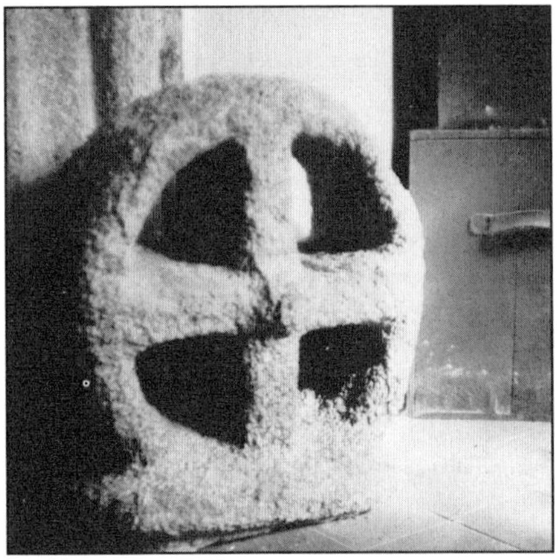

SX 3554, 8235 - Lawhitton churchtown is situated 2 1/2 miles south-east of the market town of Launceston. Access - When the parish church is unlocked.

This fine four holed cross head leans against a column in the parish church on the south side of the chancel. The cross head was discovered built into an old barn at Tregada Farm in the parish. In 1883, when the building was demolished, the stone was purchased by Mrs. Morshead of Treniffle for ten shillings and placed in her garden for preservation. Here the monument stood until 1913, when it was removed to the churchyard and placed above the Morshead family grave. In recent years the cross head has again been shifted, this time into the church where it is now protected from the weather.

The cross itself is similar in design to the crosses at Michaelstow and Laneast churchyards, all three display an abacus (a type of collar) at the neck of the monument. The head is smaller than the Michaelstow cross, its limbs are parallel rather than expanded which, with the outer ring creates four large triangular holes. In the centre of the limbs there is a central boss, which is not present on the Michaelstow and Laneast crosses.

Ellis suggested that although the cross head was found a mile from the parish church, it was probably the original churchyard cross. The stone is far too elaborate to have been used as a simple wayside cross or bound stone.

Height 1' 11" (0.585M), Width of head 1' 7" (0.48M), Width of shaft 1' 1 1/2" (0.345M), Thickness 8" (0.2M)

68

St. Michael's Churchyard
St. Michael's Lesnewth
WHEEL HEADED WAYSIDE CROSS

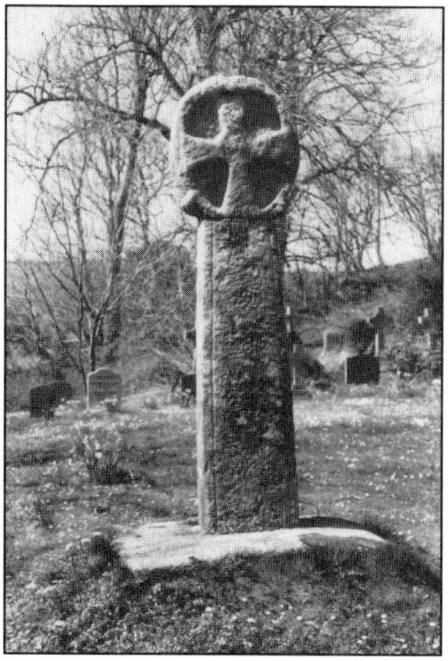

SX 1306, 9030 - St. Michael's Church is situated in a valley, 2 1/2 miles due east of Boscastle and 3/4 of a mile south of St. Juliot Church. Access - Unlimited.

On entering the churchyard the cross will be seen standing on a mound of soil adjacent to a small footbridge, which carries the church path south towards Tregrylls Farm. On examining the cross head it will soon become apparent that the head has been hollowed out on one side. In the 1860s a neighbouring farmer, after discovering the cross head, decided to hollow out one side of the stone and use it as a feeding bowl for his pigs. On attempting this, he found that the monument was not sufficiently thick enough for this purpose and the stone was later discarded.

In 1872 the cross head was rescued and eventually re-erected on a modern shaft and base stone. There are at least three other cross heads in the county which have suffered a similar fate and were hollowed out for use as feeding troughs; at Sithney, Breage and Altarnun.

Height (complete monument) 7' 5" (2.26M), Height of head 2' 5" (0.74M), Width of head 2' 2" (0.66M), Thickness 7 1/2" (0.19M).

69

Tregrylls Cross
St. Michael's Lesnewth
LATIN WAYSIDE CROSS

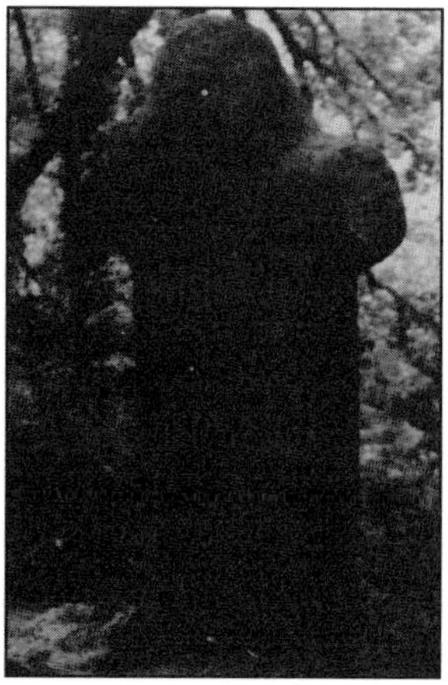

SX 1269, 8944 - The cross stands beside the old church path, in the woods below Tregrylls Farm, 3/4 mile south of Lesnewth churchtown. Access - The monument is on a public footpath (the church path) so can be viewed, although the surrounding woodland is private.

This fine Latin cross was discovered in 1988 in use as a gatepost and buried head down in the ground beside the steep sloping track below the farm. The stone had been unearthed by recent erosion, revealing its true identity.

The Latin cross has stunted upper and horizontal limbs of irregular size and length, its shaft has a massive girth of almost four feet (1.2 metres) around. The whole of the existing monument is in a good state of preservation, the shaft is worn smooth with no sharp edges. One of the horizontal limbs is slightly chipped and the cross is minus its tenon and base stone. In June 1991 the author, along with colleagues, re-erected the cross close to its existing site. When the stone was cleaned, a Latin cross in relief could just be discerned on each face, although very worn. Unfortunately the shaft of the monument had to be sunk into the ground almost two and a half feet (0.76 metres) to secure the stone safely, thus reducing its overall height. The shaft still displays evidence of its former use, having leaded holes and an iron gate hanging scarring the shaft.

Height (before erection) 6' 6 1/2" (2M), Height (after erection) 4' (1.22M), Width of shaft 1' 3" to 1' 4" (0.38M to 0.41M), Thickness of shaft 6" to 8 1/2" (0.15M to 0.22M)

70

Cross Hill
St. Mabyn

WHEEL HEADED WAYSIDE CROSS

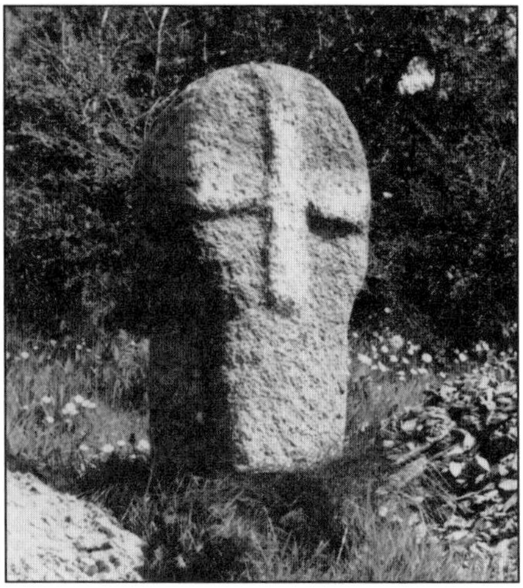

SX 0459, 7448 - One mile due north from St. Mabyn churchtown, on the road to St. Tudy. Access - The cross stands on private ground, there is no public access.

This monument stands at Cross Hill, where the road from St. Mabyn to St. Tudy is joined by another from Dinhams Bridge. Here in front of a cottage, stands a small wayside cross with its limbs painted white, similar to the Whitecross at St. Breock.

In the latter part of the last century it was standing in a field, close to the hedge and opposite the cottage. Langdon considered it to be *in situ* when it was in the field, although the author considers that it more likely stood on the grass island at the road junction.

In 1913 the owner of the cottage, Mr. Warne, removed the stone, intending to erect it on the wastrel, but due to the outbreak of the First World War the job was not completed until 1935. It is only since this date that the stone has been painted white, a practice started by Mr. Warne.

The cross could be viewed from the public road until 1989 when regrettably a high garden wall was built, concealing it from public view.

Height 3' (0.92M), Width of shaft 11" (0.28M), Width of head 1' 4" (0.405M), Thickness 9 1/2" (0.24M).

71

Lane End Cross
St. Mabyn

WHEEL HEADED WAYSIDE CROSS

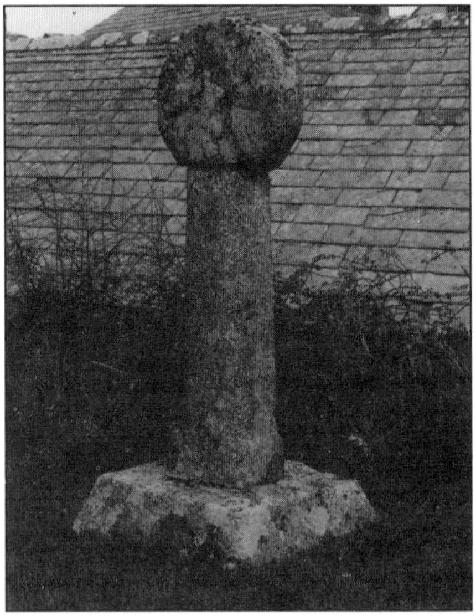

SX 0421, 7319 - On the eastern side of St. Mabyn churchyard. St. Mabyn churchtown is situated 3 1/2 miles north-east of Wadebridge. Access - Unlimited.

Maclean first recorded this cross head on the left-hand side of the road, leading from the churchtown to Longstone, which is known as Lane End. He illustrated it with what appeared to be half a base stone beside it, which has since been lost. The cross head was removed to the churchyard in 1885 and re-erected on a modern shaft with chamfered angles. The base stone is also a modern addition. The cross head is very worn.

It displays an equal limbed cross with expanded ends on each face and is enclosed in a narrow bead which is barely discernible.

Height (complete monument) 6' 4 1/2" (1.94M), Height of head 1' 8" (0.51M), Width of head 1' 11" (0.58M).

72

Penwine Cross
Longstone, St. Mabyn
WHEEL HEADED WAYSIDE CROSS

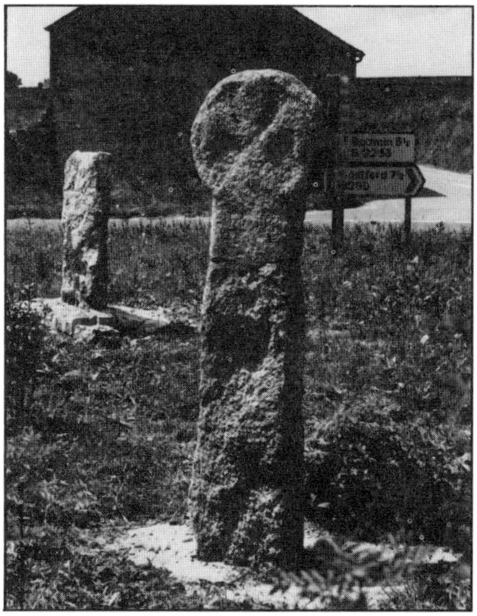

SX 0607, 7337 - 1 1/4 miles due east of St. Mabyn churchtown adjacent to the B.3266 Bodmin to Camelford road, where the ancient road from St. Mabyn to Blisland crosses it. Access - Unlimited.

The Penwine Cross stands on the wastrel close to a prehistoric Longstone (which gives its name to the village) and a 19th century direction post. Penwine Farm lies a quarter of a mile east of Longstone on the left-hand side of the road towards Blisland. When the cross head was seen by Langdon only a small amount of shaft existed, and the stone was cemented to a farmyard wall. In 1947 the Wadebridge Old Cornwall Society visited Penwine Farm and made arrangements with the owner Mrs. Warne to re-erect the stone at Longstone crossroads, where the base of a cross still exists.

Unfortunately the monument was not erected at the crossroads until 1969, when the head was mounted on a newly cut shaft and base stone by De Lank stone masons at St. Breward. The most interesting feature about this cross is the fact that it bears the fleur-de-lys symbol on one face, similar to the Priors Cross (see No. 32 in this guide). The reverse face displays an equal limbed Greek style cross.

Height (complete) 6' 1" (1.855M), Height of original cross head 2' 4" (0.71M), Width of head 1' 9" (0.53M), Thickness 6" 1/2" (0.165M).

73

Longstone Cross Base
St. Mabyn
BASE OF WAYSIDE CROSS

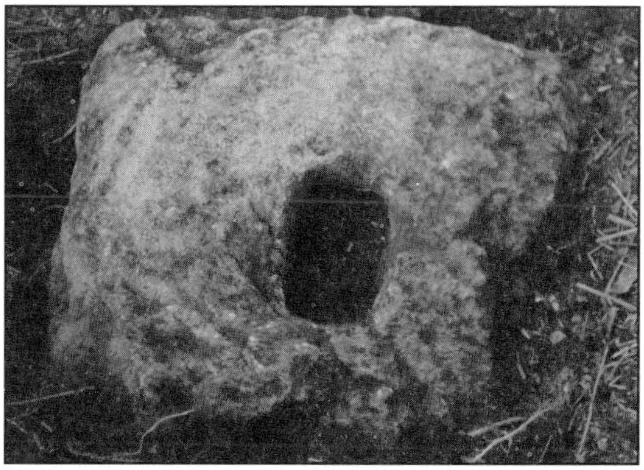

SX 0609, 7388 - Lying down, concealed by vegetation 12 metres north-east of Penwine Cross (No. 72 in this guide). Access - Unlimited.

The existence of a cross base near the Longstone has been known for some years and Ellis recorded that he hoped that the old base stone would be utilised in the restored Penwine Cross. Today the old base stone lies half buried in the wastrel near the Longstone and the Penwine Cross. Viewing the stone is difficult as the ground nearby has been used for dumping rubbish over a period of years.

In 1947 the base was built into the wall adjacent to the wastrel in a vertical position but in recent years the stone has been removed and now lies in a horizontal position.

3' 1" by 2' 9" by 9 1/2" (0.94M by 0.84M by 0.24M), Mortice 10 1/2" by 6 1/2" (0.265M by 0.16M).

74

Tresloggett Cross
St. Mabyn
WHEEL HEADED WAYSIDE OR BOUNDARY CROSS

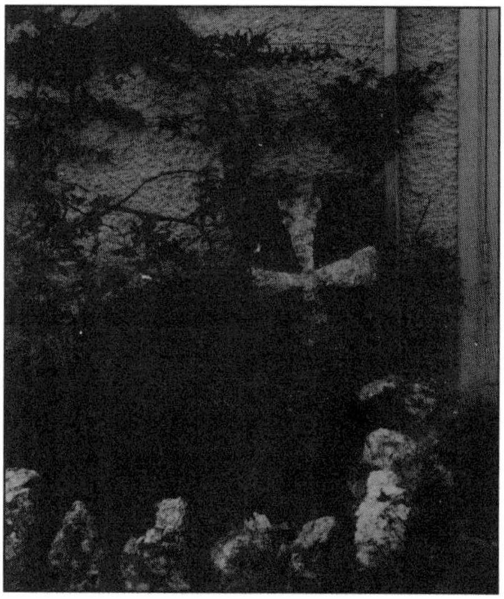

SX 0699, 7334 - In the garden of Tregony Farm (formerly known as Tresloggett), on the road between Longstone and Tresarrett. Access - The cross is on private ground, there is no public access.

This ancient stone was found during road improvements in 1939. It was discovered together with a small portion of shaft, in a hedge opposite the farm entrance. The hedge on the northern side of the road is the parish boundary between St. Tudy and St. Mabyn. Ellis suggested that the cross may have stood at Three Turnings, a junction 200 yards to the east, which led north to Penhale and St. Tudy churchtown. There the monument would have served as both a wayside guide and also a parish boundary stone. The mutilated monument known as Tresloggett Cross was originally round headed with an equal limbed cross upon each face. The head was at some time hacked off in line with the shaft and used as a gatepost, being later discarded in the hedge.

Height 2' 3" (0.68M), Width of head 13" (0.33M), Width of head (originally) 1' 6" (0.46M), Width of shaft 11" (0.28M), Thickness 4 1/2" to 6" (0.11M to 0.15M).

75

Boconnion Cross
Colquite, St. Mabyn
WHEEL HEADED WAYSIDE CROSS

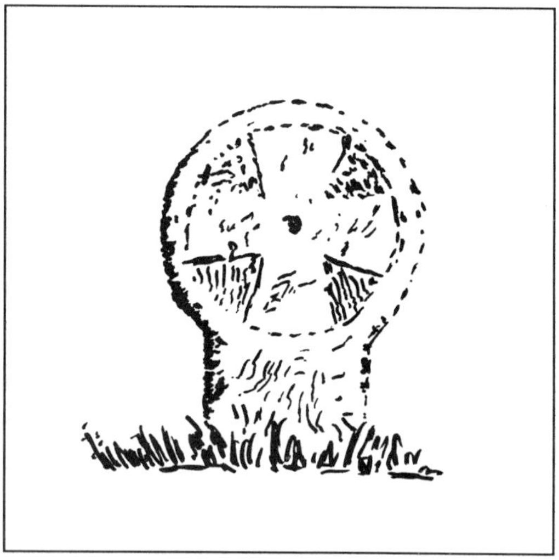

SX 0539, 7085 - In the garden of Colquite Farm, 2 miles south-east of St. Mabyn churchtown. Access - The monument is on private property and there is no public access.

For many years this round headed cross was built into the threshold of a doorway to a cows' house at Boconnion in the parish of Helland. The monument's previous history is unknown; it was removed to Colquite prior to 1881. The stone displays an equal limbed cross with slightly expanded limbs on each face and with a small hole in the centre.

This cross may have once marked the ancient track from Bodmin north via Clerkenwater to Helland and been the next marker along the route from the Berry Cross (see No. 4 in this guide).

Height 1' 8 1/2" (0.52M), Width of head 1' 6 1/2" (0.47M), Width of shaft 11 1/2" (0.29M), Thickness 5 1/2" (0.14M).

76

Cross in Parish Church
Marhamchurch
LATIN CROSS

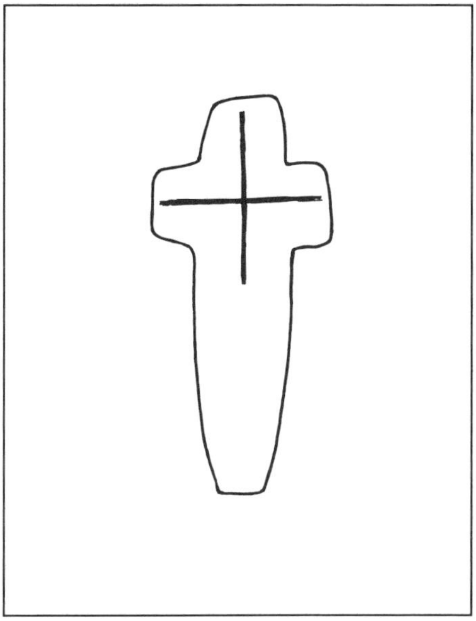

SS 2231, 0367 - The cross is in the parish church at Marhamchurch, a village 2 miles south of the coastal town of Bude. Access - The public can view the stone when the church is unlocked, normally during daylight hours.

On entering the church, this small Latin cross of granite will be seen clamped to a blind arch on the north-western wall. The monument, which has a tapered shaft and stunted horizontal limbs, displays an incised Latin cross on its face, the reverse face unfortunately cannot be examined. It has been suggested that as it was found in the churchyard, it may be an early gravestone.

Height (approx.) 1' 6" (0.46M), Width 8" (0.2M), Thickness 3" (0.075).

77

Base Stone in Churchyard
St. Merryn
GOTHIC CROSS BASE

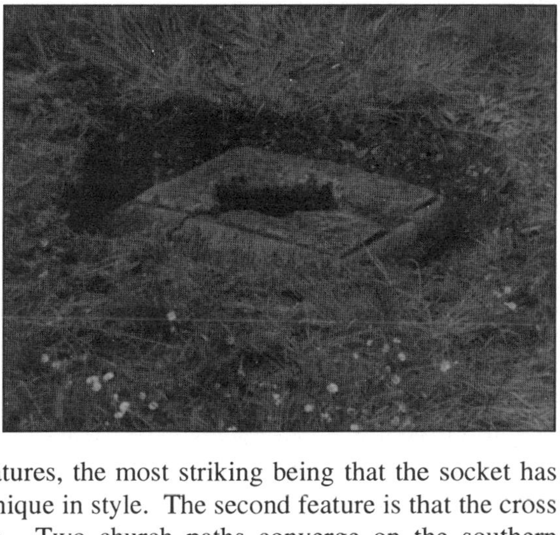

SW 8864, 7412 - The stone lies half covered by turf on the south side of the churchyard, directly in line with the church porch, and close to the grave stone of John G. Hawke and his wife. Access - Unlimited.

Langdon recorded the existence of a circular cross base on the south side of this churchyard. In 1958 Mary Henderson, while searching for this cross base, discovered a rectangular base stone but was unable to find the stone Langdon noted.

The cross base has two unusual features, the most striking being that the socket has been cut diagonally on the stone making it unique in style. The second feature is that the cross base has a rebate around its upper surface. Two church paths converge on the southern boundary of the churchyard, one from Kerketh and another from Trevorgus, each could have been marked by a cross. The stone is cut from local Cateclewse greenstone from the medieval coastal quarry near Trevose Head in the parish.

2' 6" by 2' 4 1/2" (0.76M by. 725M), Thickness 7" (0.18M), Mortice 1' 1 1/2" (0.345M), Depth of Mortice 6" (0.15M) by 8" (0.2M).

78

Tresallyn Cross
St. Merryn
GOTHIC LATIN CROSS

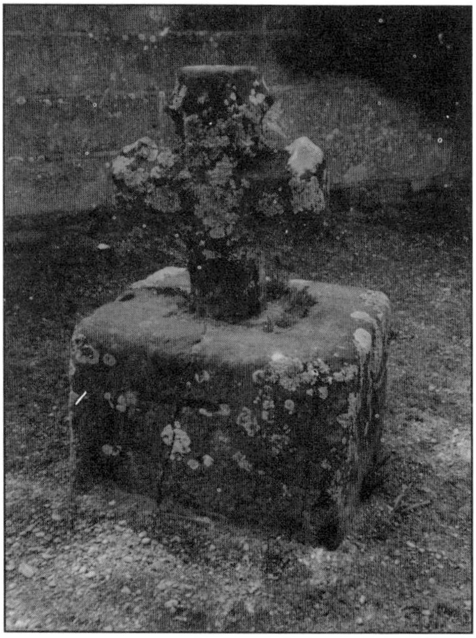

SX 8930, 7326 - In the garden of Tresallyn Farmhouse, approximately half a mile south-east of the parish church. Access - The monument is on private ground, there is no public access.

This Latin cross displays cusps between its limbs, which indicates that it is from the late Gothic period. Langdon noted the stone's existence, Baird suggested that at one time the monument stood at the nearby Tresallyn crossroads, although it appears far too decorative to be a wayside cross.

There is no previous history known about the stone's original purpose, although it may have been connected with one of the many ancient chapels in the area. The cross is cut from local Cateclewse greenstone.

Height 1' 9" (0.53M), Width across head 1' 5 1/2" (0.45M).

79

Trevenning Cross
Michaelstow
FOUR HOLED CROSS
possibly BOUNDARY CROSS

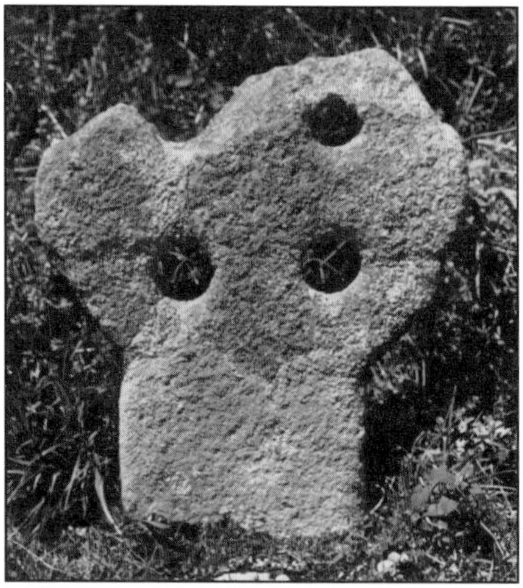

SX 0736, 7747 - Adjacent to the B3266 Bodmin to Camelford road on a sharp right-hand bend, where a minor road continues straight on towards Treveighan. On the boundary of St. Tudy and Michaelstow parishes. Access - Unlimited;

This cross was discovered directly behind its present position and had received much damage. A base stone removed from Tregawn Gate in Michaelstow by Mr. J.R. Collins of Bodmin was used to support the four holed cross. This indicates the possibility of another cross still to be found in the area. When Langdon examined the stone he found it had recently been fractured, resulting in only one hole being intact. He recorded the cross under the parish of St. Tudy rather than Michaelstow.

Ellis did not support the theory that the stone once marked the parish boundary as the stone is not mentioned in the 1613 Terrier. It would have been unusual for an elaborate stone such as a four holed cross to be used as a simple bound stone or guidepost. Ellis suggested it was used between the two ecclesiastic centres of Bodmin and St. Teath as a preaching cross.

Height 2' 6" (0.76M), Width of head 1' 11" (0.58M), Thickness 6" (0.15M), Width of shaft 1' 1" (0.33M), Base stone 3' 6" (1.07M), in length, Base stone 7" (0.18M), deep.

80

Churchyard Cross
Michaelstow
FOUR HOLED CHURCHYARD CROSS

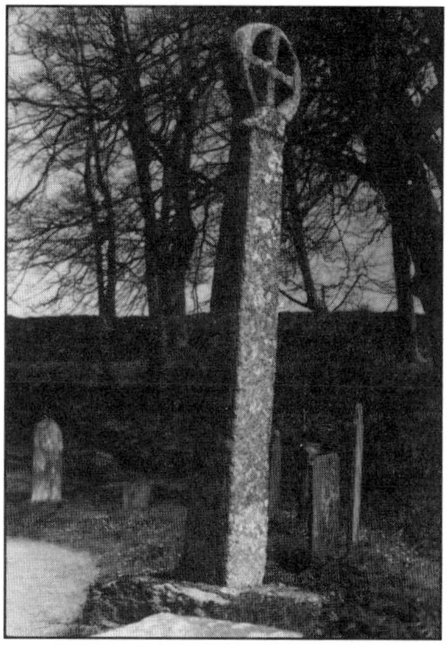

SX 0807, 7885 - On the south-western side of Michaelstow churchyard, the churchtown is 4 miles south-west of Camelford. Access - Unlimited.

Here in Michaelstow churchyard is a finely executed medieval four holed cross of elegant proportions. Prior to 1883, the shaft with a fragment of cross head attached, was in use as the bottom step in a flight leading up to the western side of the raised churchyard. The remaining fragment of cross head was found close by and the monument was later skilfully renovated and re-erected in the churchyard. It appears likely that this was the original churchyard cross.

Langdon recorded the stone under the heading, "four holed cross with an Abacus". An abacus in architectural terms, is the collar like disc which can be seen at the neck of the cross. He only recorded two examples under this heading, the second was at Lawhitton and since then a third at Laneast has also been discovered.

Height 11' 2" (3.4M), Width of head 2' 3" (0.68M), Width of shaft 1' to 1' 5" (0.3M to 0.43M), Thickness of shaft 7" (0.18M)

81

Trevenning No. 1
Michaelstow
WHEEL HEADED WAYSIDE CROSS

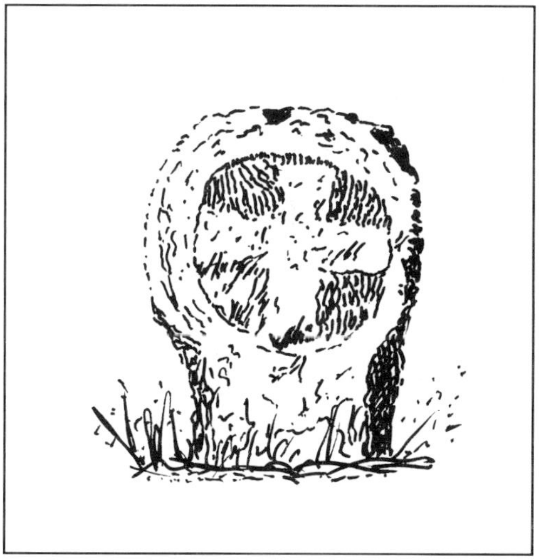

SX 0795, 7808 - In the private grounds of Trevennen House, Trevenning. The hamlet of Trevenning is situated 3/4 of a mile south of Michaelstow Church. Access -The monument is on private grounds, there is no public access.

Originally three cross heads were recorded at Trevennen, but later one was discovered to be the base stone of a cheese press. Langdon recorded that they were removed by the former owner, Mr. Bastard, from the moors near Roughtor in 1888.

The two authentic crosses are different (see No. 82 in this guide). The first of the two stones has a broad limbed cross in relief of irregular size, enclosed in a narrow bead and is rather chipped. The short portion of shaft is rebated on the sides instead of having a raised bead, which may suggest a transition towards a chamfered edge. The cross head sits in a base stone, which Langdon stated was also removed from the moors, but indicated that the two old stones were parts of separate monuments.

Height 2' 3" (0.68M), Width of head 1' 10" (0.56M), Width of shaft 1' 5" (0.43M), Base stone 3' 4" by 2' 11" by 7" (1.01M by 0.89M by 0.18M).

Trevenning No. 2
Michaelstow
WHEEL HEADED WAYSIDE CROSS

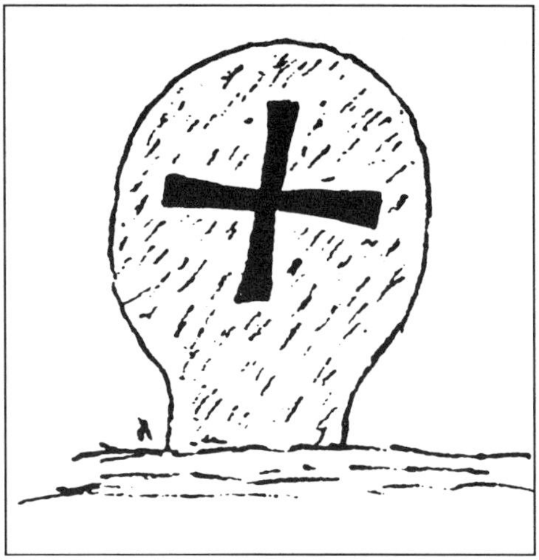

SX 0795, 7808 - In the private grounds of Trevennen House, Trevenning. Access - The monument is on private grounds, there is no public access.

The second of these small crosses (see No. 81 in this guide) displays an incised cross on either face, with expanded ends, one of which is inclined slightly. Again, only a small amount of shaft remain. A third stone built into a wall above a door to the side of the entrance to the property is actually the base stone of a cheese press.

Height 1' 6 1/2" (0.47M), Width of head 1' 5" (0.43M), Width of shaft 11" (0.28M), Thickness 6 1/2" (0.16M)

83

Waterpit Down Cross Shaft
Minster
SHAFT OF POSSIBLE CHURCHYARD OR PREACHING CROSS

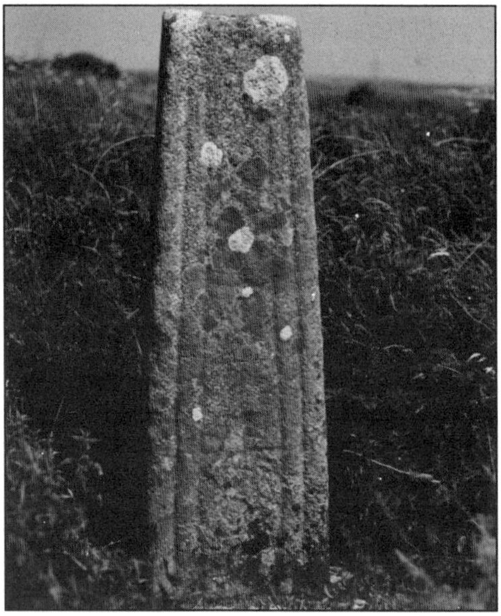

SX 1120, 8806 - 3/4 mile east from the B3266 Camelford to Boscastle road, 3 1/2 miles north of Camelford town. Access - Unlimited.

When Maclean visited Waterpit Down in the early 1870s only the massive cross base existed at the site and he recorded that the cross shaft had been removed to Trekeek Farm in approximately 1853. At Trekeek, which is situated about half a mile south of the site, the cross shaft was used as the base stone or pivot for a horse drawn threshing machine and was illustrated by Langdon in this position. The cross shaft remained at Trekeek until June 1889, when it was replaced in its socket again, due to the effort of Colonel S.G. Blake of Camelford.

The cross shaft is decorated on all four sides, although some of the detail appears to have been erased by the weather. The monument is also inscribed with an Hiberno Saxon inscription *CRVX INBVRGE* and was translated by the Rev. William Iago to read "The Cross of Inburga". A leaded hole still exists in the shaft where the iron pivot was fixed. Above, in the top of the shaft, is a mortice to which a cross head must have once been fastened. Maclean suggested that the missing head was possibly the cross head at St. Michael's, Lesnewth, but Langdon disagreed, stating that the style of cross shaft suggested a four holed cross head.

Height 7' 5" (2.26M), Width of shaft (top) 1' 5 1/2"(0.44M), Width of shaft (bottom) 2' 2" (0.66M), Thickness 10 1/2" to 11" (0.26M to 0.28M), Base stone 5' square (1.52M) 11" deep (0.28M), Mortice in the top of the shaft 6" dia. (0.15M)

84

Treglines Cross
St. Minver Highlands
LATIN WAYSIDE CROSS

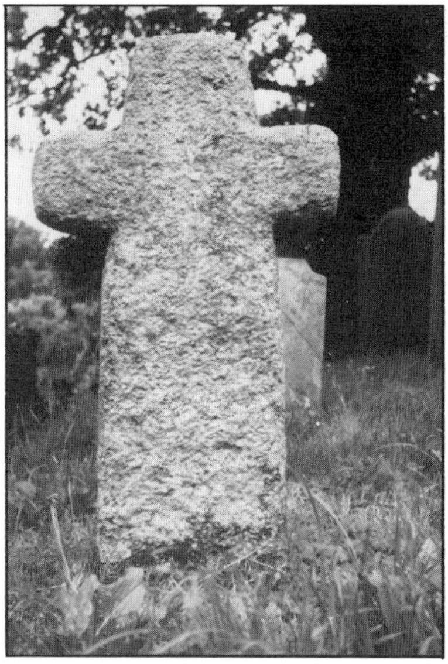

SW 9648, 7708 - This cross stands near the south porch of St. Minver Church. St. Minver churchtown is 4 miles north-west of Wadebridge, along the B3314 road. Access - Unlimited

This small Latin cross once stood in a field at Treglines Farm, close to the old Quaker burial ground and was used by cattle as a rubbing post. Treglines Farm lies one mile north-west of the parish churchyard and, according to Ellis, lay on an ancient track used by fishermen walking between St. Enodoc and Port Isaac. This track originally ran from St. Enodoc, via Roserrow and Treglines to Trevigo and from there via Sarrabine and Roscarrock to the fishing village of Port Isaac. The cross may have been used as a medieval route marker along this track and could have also guided the way to Roserrow where, during the 15th century, an ancient chapel existed.

In 1879 the monument was removed to the churchyard, where it remains in a good state of preservation.

Height 2' 10" (0.86M), Width of head 1' 7" (0.48M), Thickness 6" (0.15M)

85

St. Enodoc Church
St. Minver Lowlands
WHEEL HEADED WAYSIDE CROSS

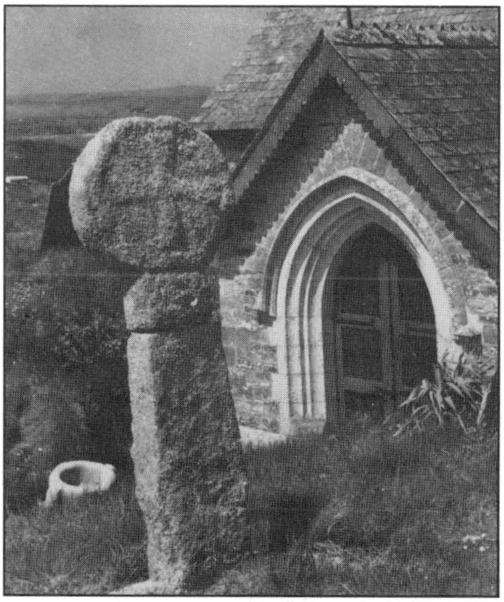

SW 9316, 7722 - Inside the church porch at St. Enodoc Church. Take the B3314 road to St. Minver and minor road to Daymer Bay via. Trebetherick. From Daymer Bay the visitor has a 1/4 mile walk across the golf links to the church. Access - The church porch is normally open during hours of daylight.

The cross today is protected from the weather and stands fixed to the inside wall of the church porch. Blight illustrated the cross head leaning in the churchyard, but later Langdon recorded both the head and upper portion of shaft built into the churchyard wall, when the church was restored in 1863. The monument displays an equal limbed cross in relief with slightly expanded ends enclosed in a narrow bead. The reverse face is said to be similar, but is now hidden from view. The cross was restored by the late Mr. F.J. Hext of Tredethy. This photograph shows the monument prior to being removed to the porch.

Height 5' 8 1/2" (1.74M), Width of head 1' 10" (0.56M), Width of shaft 10" to 1' 1" (0.25M to 0.33M), Thickness 6" (0.15M).

86

St. Michael's Porthilly Churchyard St. Minver Lowlands

FOUR HOLED CHURCHYARD OR PREACHING CROSS

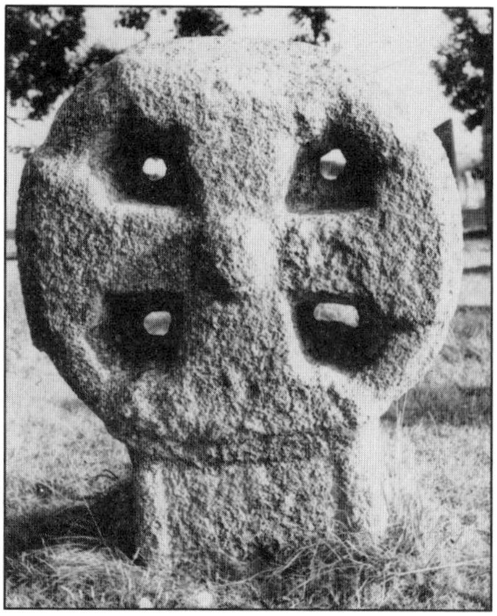

SW 9367, 7534 - On the south side of St. Michael's Churchyard. The churchyard is situated at Porthilly Cove near the village of Rock. Access to the churchyard is via the farmyard from Porthilly Lane. Access - Unlimited.

There is no record of when this massive four holed cross was discovered, although Maclean suggested that it was removed from the western side of the church. The granite monument's four holes have been pierced through from both faces and are not uniform in size. There is a central boss on the front face and all four sides of the shaft display decoration. If this cross was complete with its shaft and base stone, it would have been a monument of considerable height. A recent paper on the Porthilly Cross suggests that it may be connected with the shaft of the Padstow Cross Shaft (see No. 89 in this guide), although this has not been proved conclusively.

Height 3' 6" (1.067M), Width of head 2' 9" (0.84M), Width of shaft 1' 7" (0.48M), Thickness 11 1/2" (0.29M).

87

Tonacombe Cross Morwenstow

WHEEL HEADED WAYSIDE CROSS

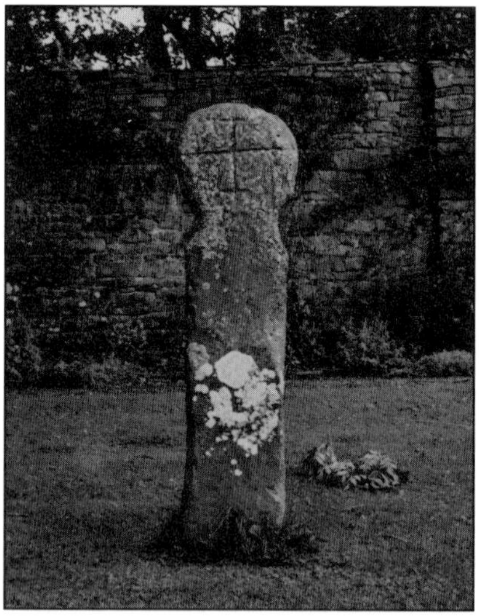

SS 2090, 1455- The cross stands in a secluded garden, in the grounds of Tonacombe Manor. Access - There is no public access, the monument is on private property.

According to the late Charles Henderson, this cross was discovered in September 1918, buried head down in the ground, and in use as a rubbing post in a field to the north of the manor house. Its former site with all probability was on the old church path, marking the route from Tonacombe north-west to Morwenstow church. There are three unusual features about this stone; i) that it is the most easterly wheel cross in Cornwall until 1918, the nearest wheel cross to Devon was at Laneast, ii) the monument is cut from grey elvan stone, locally known as cliff stone, the majority are cut from granite and, iii) the stone displays an incised cross-crosslet on each face, a style unique on Cornish crosses. Ellis suggested that the monument was a relatively late style of wheel cross, dating from the end of the 12th century.

Height 5' 2" (1.58M), Width of head 1' 3 1/2" (0.39M), Width of shaft 1' 1" (0.33M), Thickness 6" (0.15M).

88

Churchyard Cross Shaft
Padstow

SHAFT OF PREACHING OR CHURCHYARD CROSS

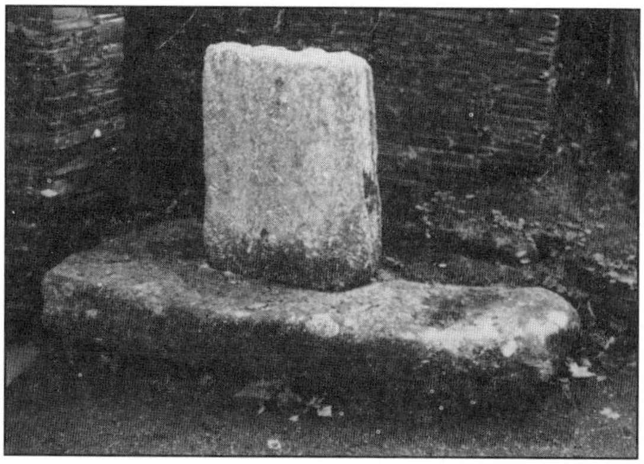

SW 9160, 7539 - Beside the south-eastern gate to Padstow churchyard. Access - Unlimited.

This enormous cross shaft and its base stone were discovered in 1869 while the parish sexton was digging the grave for William Sowden, and was found just 18 inches (0.46M) under the surface. It appears likely that the monument, which would have been of a considerable height, had become fractured and that the remaining shaft and base were covered over the years due to interments.

Langdon also recorded that a sexton digging the grave for a Molly Waters, also on the south side of the churchyard, discovered the head of a cross, but at the time it was not considered worthwhile to be retrieved and the burial went ahead.

The shaft is decorated on all four sides with interlace work, plaitwork and a possible fleur-de-lys. It was due to members of the Prideaux Brune family that the ancient stone was rescued and preserved in the churchyard.

Height of shaft 3' 6" (1.067M), Width of shaft (top) 2' 6" (0.76M), Width of shaft (bottom) 3' (0.91M), Thickness of shaft 1'1" (0.33M), Length of base stone 8' (2.44M), Width of base stone 5' (1.524M), Thickness of base stone 1' 1" (0.33M).

89

Padstow Churchyard Cross
Padstow

FOUR HOLED CHURCHYARD OR PREACHING CROSS

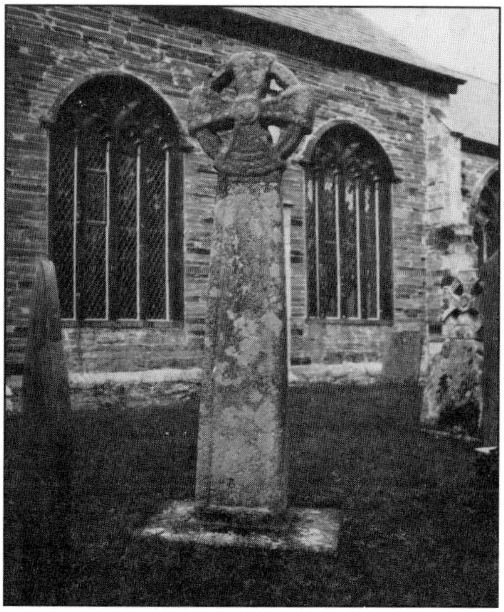

SW 9156, 7539 - Right-hand side of the south porch of the parish church. Access - Unlimited.

This four holed cross is the smallest of its type in the Duchy. The cross head, which was cut from a piece of grey elvan stone, was removed from a garden wall adjoining the churchyard. The cross head had been used as a simple building stone in the wall and Langdon stated that the holes of the cross had been filled with mortar and pieces of brick. The garden wall was formerly the boundary of the old Vicarage, which had long since been demolished.

The stone was re-erected on a modern shaft and base stone in 1897 by Mr. Downey., a stonemason from Bodmin, at the expense of Mr. C.G. Prideaux-Brune.

Height or original cross head and shaft 1' 11" (0.59M), Width of head 1' 8 1/2" (0.52M), Width of shaft 7" (0.28M), Thickness of head 5" (0.13M), Height of complete monument 6' 3 1/2" (1.92M).

90

Prideaux Brune Vault
Padstow

GOTHIC LATIN CROSS

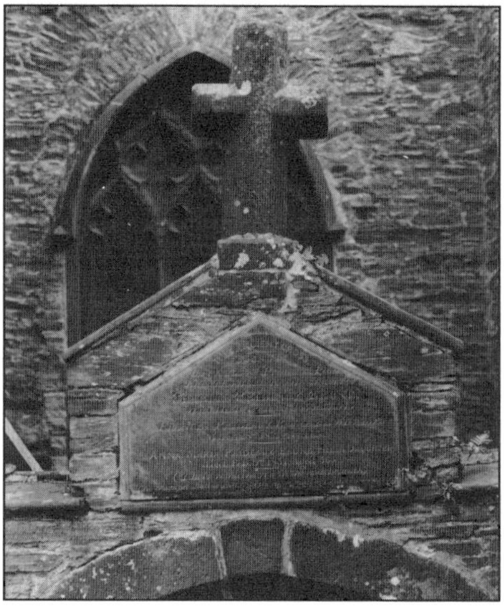

SW 9155, 7541 - On the western side of the church close to the tower in Padstow churchyard. The cross is fixed to a gable above a doorway to the vault. Access - Unlimited.

This Gothic Latin cross is octagonal in section and a plaque below it reads that it was discovered in the grounds of Prideaux Place, a manor house at the top of Padstow town. Prideaux Place is a site of great antiquity and was acquired by the Prideaux family at the time of the dissolution of the monasteries. The Elizabethan manor was built in the latter part of the 16th century. The site of an ancient hermitage or chapel of St. Samson is also said to exist in the grounds. According to Henderson, in the 18th century there stood the ruins of no less than seven ancient chapels in Padstow and this gable cross may have been attached to one of these.

Height 1' 8" (0.51M), Width of shaft 7" (0.18M), Width of head 1' (0.305M), Thickness 7" (0.18M).

91

Prideaux Place Cross
Padstow

FOUR HOLED PREACHING OR MONASTIC CROSS

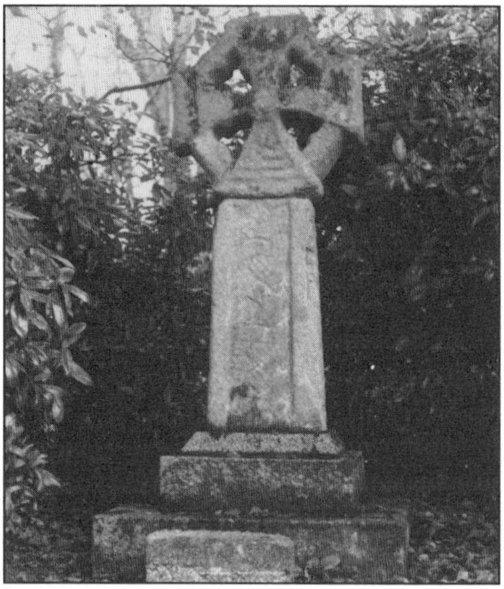

SW 9130, 7553 - On the edge of the lawn on the south-west side of Prideaux Place manor house. The manor house is situated 1/4 mile north-west of the church. Access - the house and grounds are open to the public throughout the summer and also by appointment. (There is no free access to the crosses only).

The cross head stood in the gardens for many years and Mr. Charles Prideaux-Brune found a small length of the original shaft and had the two joined and mounted on a stepped base.

In 1974 another fragment of the cross shaft was discovered by Canadian student Lynette Olson beneath the roots of a tree in the woods behind the manor. In 1987 the tree was felled and the fragment was rescued by the author and placed by the existing monument. The author is convinced that there are still more fragments of the shaft hidden in the grounds awaiting discovery.

The head of the monument is unusual, being almost octagonal in shape due to the ends of the limbs being flat. The shaft is ornamented on all four sides and consists of figure of eight knotwork, scrollwork and plaitwork.

Height 6' 1" (1.85M), Width of head 2' 9" (0.84M), Width of shaft (top) 1' 4" (0.41M), Width of shaft (bottom) 1' 8" (0.51M), Thickness of head 11" (0.28M), Thickness of shaft 1' (0.305M), Fragment length 1' 9" (0.53M), Fragment width 10 1/2" to 11 1/2" (0.265M to 0.29M), Fragment thickness 1' to 1' 1" (0.305 to 0.33M).

92

Deer Park Cross
Prideaux Place, Padstow
SEMI-GOTHIC LATIN CROSS

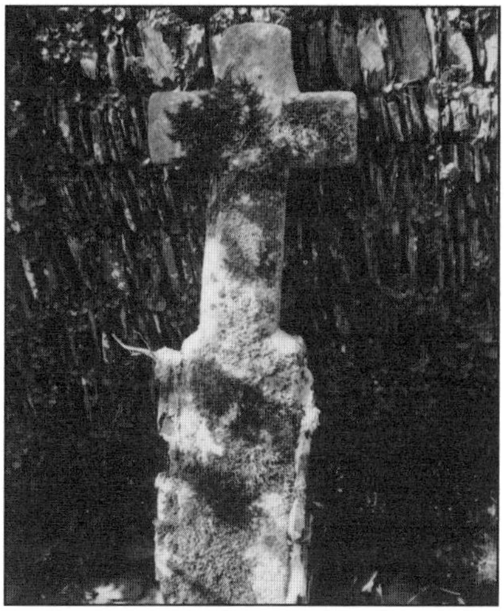

SW 9146, 7570 - Against a hedge near the entrance to the Deer Park. Access - At present inaccessible. The house and grounds are open to the public throughout the summer and also by appointment. (There is no free access to view the crosses only).

This small Latin cross has chamfered sides which makes it octagonal, and is cemented onto an additional piece of stone. The cross has been placed below the high stone hedge of the Deer Park to the north-east of the manor house. The limbs of the monument are slightly crooked and have been fractured in the past and later repaired. The monument is slightly taller than the Prideaux-Brune vault cross in the churchyard, making it difficult to decide whether it was originally a gable cross or a free-standing cross.

Height 2')0.61M), Width of head 1' 3 1/2" (0.39M), Width of shaft 5 1/2" (0.14M), Width of limbs 5" (0.125M), Thickness of cross 4 1/2" (0.115M).

93

Holyway (Holloway) Cross
South Petherwin
WHEEL HEADED WAYSIDE CROSS

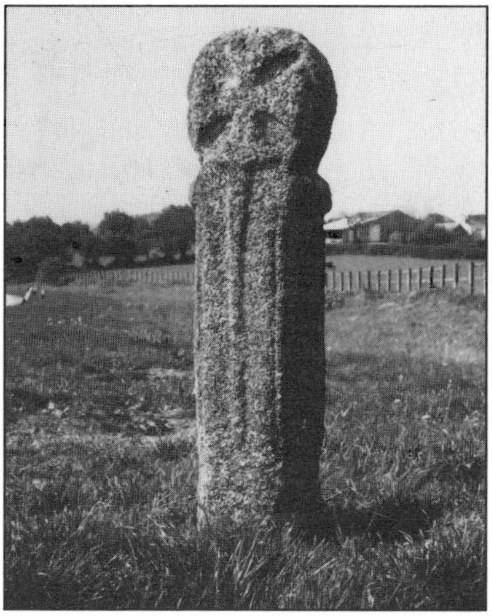

SX 2727, 8232 - Stands beside the A30 trunk road from Bodmin to Launceston, 4 miles south-west of Launceston town. Access - Unlimited.

This cross was discovered by Col. C. Archer of Trelaske, Lewannick, many years ago and was built into a hedge almost opposite its present site. The stone was preserved in the garden of a cottage which, until the end of the Second World War, stood at the road junction. During the war the cottage was badly damaged when an army lorry ran into it. Later it was demolished and the cross was left lying on the newly made wastrel, formerly the site of the cottage, and later in 1950 was re-erected by Launceston Old Cornwall Society in conjunction with the County Council.

The monument displays an equal limbed cross with widely expanded ends, the sides of the limbs being concave. The lower limb has an extended bead or band carved in relief continuing down the centre of the shaft to within a foot of the base stone. At the neck of the cross are two rounded projections with a narrow bead running down the sides of the shaft to the base.

When the stone was situated in the garden it was deeply buried without a base stone and measured only 3' 7" (1.09M) in height. It is now re-erected on a new base stone and can be seen at its true height.

Height (above base stone) 5' 3" (1.6M), Width of head 1' 10" (0.56M), Width of shaft (at neck) 1' 5" (0.43M), Width of shaft (at base) 1' 3" (0.38M), Thickness 6" to 8 1/2" (0.15 to 0.215M).

94

Maer Farm Cross
Poughill
WHEEL HEADED CROSS

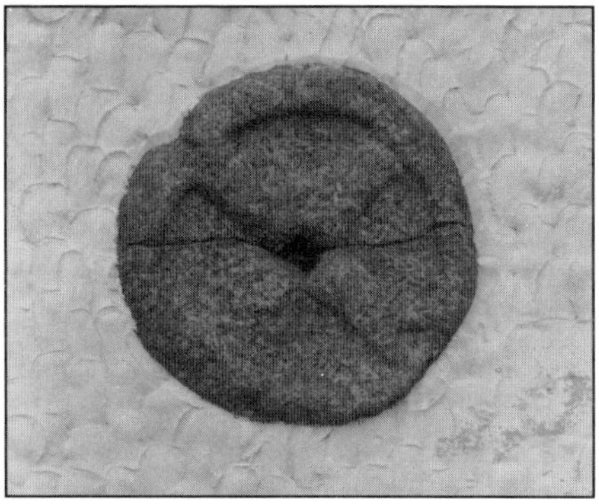

SS 2076, 0791 - Maer Farm is situated 1 mile to the north of Bude town near the coast. Access - The stone can be easily viewed from the public roadside, it is built into the wall of a private dwelling.

The cross head will be found built into a converted barn on the opposite side of the road to a farmhouse. Until recent years the stone stood on a rough granite shaft beside the road. The cross head has a square hole cut through its centre which has fractured the stone, thus suggesting that it may have once been used for some agricultural or mechanical purpose.

Diameter 1' 9 1/2" (0.55M), Bead 3" (0.07M), Thickness unknown.

95

St. Teath Cross
St. Teath
FOUR HOLED CHURCHYARD CROSS

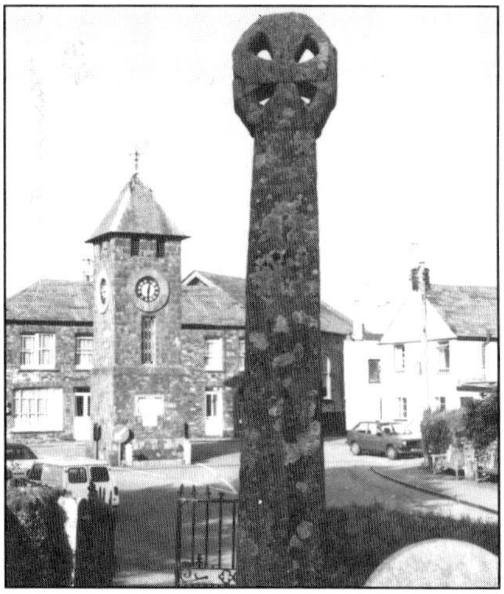

SX 0638, 8063 - At the entrance to the cemetery, close to the village clock tower and opposite St. Teath churchyard. Access - Unlimited.

In 1883 a report on this monument was printed in the Antiquarian Magazine. Here it was stated that the old stone for many years served as a footbridge across the outlet of a pond in the neighbourhood. When the cross was removed to the churchyard in 1835 the vicar found it difficult to erect the stone owing to the loss of the tenon on the bottom of the shaft and the damage to the base stone. It was some time in the next few years that the monument received its mutilation.

When the Rev. Thomas Worthington re-discovered the stone in 1883 it was in many pieces. The head was in use as a pivot for the churchyard gate, the first three feet of the shaft were chopped into one foot cubes and built into the gateway, and the remaining 8' 6" (2.6M) of shaft was cut lengthways and used as coping for the churchyard wall. All the ornamentation was erased on the lower part of the shaft when it was used for this purpose. Today the only decoration existing is some scroll work on the upper section of the shaft, and triquetra knots on each limb of the cross head. The monument is the third tallest in the Duchy, Mylor and Quethiock being higher.

During the 1980s the author became concerned that pieces of the Victorian cement repairs to the head were breaking off, due to frost and adverse weather conditions. In 1994 a restoration project was organised by Mr. David Attwell of the North Cornwall Heritage Coast & Countryside Service. In April 1995 the repairs were carried out by Somerset conservators, Sue and Lawrence Kelland, and were overseen by Ann Preston-Jones - Field Monument Warden for English Heritage.

Height (complete) 13' (3.96M), Width of head 1' 11" (0.58M), Width of shaft (top) 1' 0 1/2" (0.32M), Width of shaft (bottom) 1' 9" (0.53M), Thickness of shaft (top) 11" (0.28M), Thickness of shaft (bottom) 1' 2" (0.35M).

96

Bosinney or Fenterleigh Cross
Tintagel
WHEEL HEADED WAYSIDE CROSS

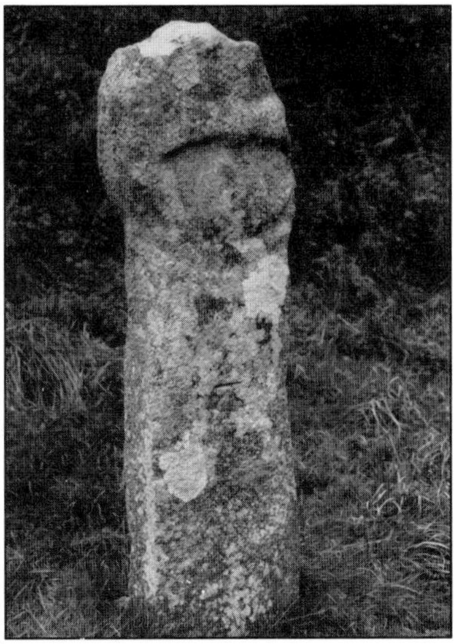

SX 0716, 8831 - This monument is situated near the village of Bosinney at a crossroads known as Fenterleigh or Pentaly, approximately 1 mile east of Tintagel. Access - Unlimited.

When this monument was recorded in the 1860s the stone was standing against a hedge and only the front of the cross was visible. In recent years, due to road alterations, the monument has been moved to a wide grass verge where examination is easy. It has been suggested that it was carved by the same hand that cut the Trevillet cross (see No. 97 in this guide) as both have similar heads, having the cross formed by cutting four triangular sinkings. Another similarity is that each stone displays a centre boss and both were discovered within half a mile of each other. Sadly, today the cross has been disfigured by the carving of an Ordnance Survey Bench Mark. The cross is not *in situ*, its base stone being missing, although it may be near its original site. Nearby fields known as cross field could refer to either the monument or the crossroads.

Height 5' 1" (1.55M), Width of head 1' 9" (0.53M), Width of shaft 1' 2" (0.36M), Thickness 6 1/2" (0.16M).

97

Trevena or Trevillet Cross
Tintagel
WHEEL HEADED INSCRIBED CROSS

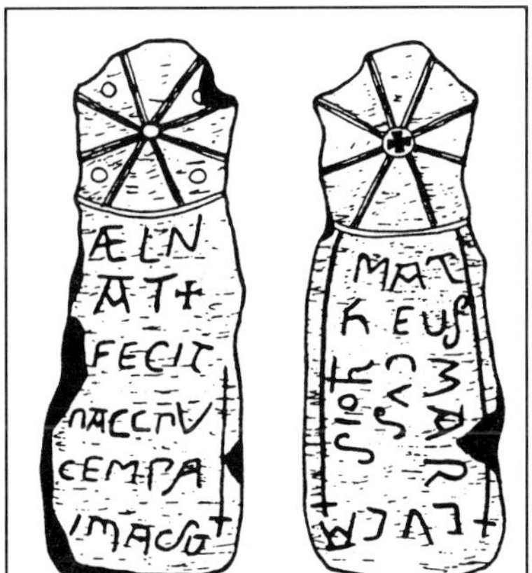

SX 0574, 8841 - The Trevillet Cross stands in a small garden in front of the Wharncliffe Arms public house. The property is in Tintagel's main street, which was formerly Trevena village. Access - The stone stands on private ground but can be easily viewed from the roadside pavement.

The Trevillet or Trevena Cross was found in use as a gatepost at Trevillet Farm and was removed to the front garden of the Wharncliffe Arms in 1875 for preservation. The stone has been badly damaged but is still of considerable interest due to its inscriptions. There are also additional features, such as five raised bosses, which are said to denote Christ's five wounds received at the Crucifixion. There is a central boss between the limbs, with an additional boss on each limb. The inscriptions read - *ALNAT FECIT HA(N) CRUCEM P(RO) A(N) IMA SU (A).* Which when translated reads "AElnat made this cross for the benefit of his soul". On the reverse face are inscribed the names of the four evangelists; Matthew, Mark, Luke and John - *MATHEUS MARCVS LUCA SIOh.* The inscriptions are in Anglo Saxon capitals and minuscules.

The stone was cut from a piece of grey elvan stone, which is a form of locally quarried greenstone.

Height 3' 10" (1.17M), Width 1' to 1' 6" (0.3M to 0.46M), Thickness 7" (0.18M)

98

Trevalga Cross
Trevalga
WHEEL HEADED WAYSIDE CROSS

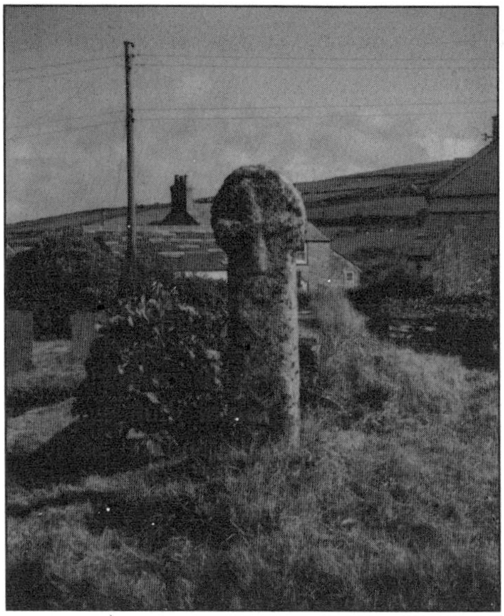

SX 0812, 9003 - Near the south side of the church, in the churchyard. Trevalga village is situated 1 1/4 miles south-west of Boscastle. Access - Unlimited.

This lichen covered monolith was, according to Polsue, once situated beside the church path and was removed to the churchyard in 1868. Langdon described it as a very early example and Ellis suggested it could be as early as the 8th century.

The stone has an equal limbed cross in relief on each face, the limbs of which, unlike most, are not expanded at their extremities. One of the crosses is also inclined considerably to the left, giving it a primitive appearance.

Height 5' 9" (1.75M), Width of shaft (top) 1' 1" (0.33M), Width of shaft (bottom) 1' 3" (0.38M), Width of head 1' 8" (0.51M), Thickness of shaft 10" (0.25M).

99

Penpol Cross
Tresmeer
LATIN WAYSIDE CROSS

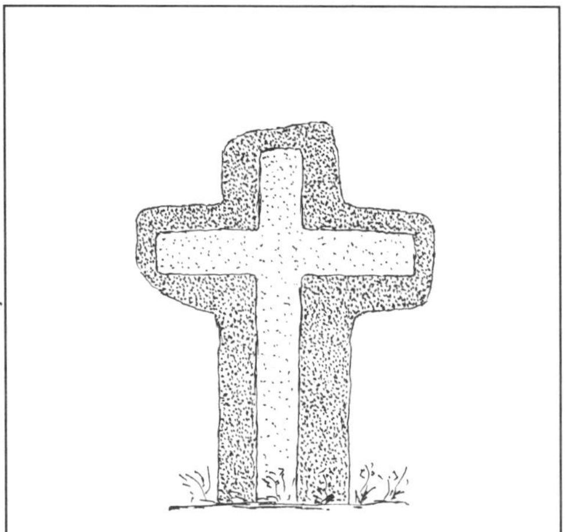

SX 2337, 8750 - The village of Tresmeer lies 7 miles north-west of Launceston and 2 1/2 miles north of Laneast churchtown. Access - Unlimited.

Blight first illustrated this cross and stated that it was deeply buried near the site of the old parsonage house at Laneast. Polsue noted that the monument was discovered in a hedge at Penpol in the parish of Laneast and was rescued by the Rev. W.A. Morgan, Vicar of Tresmeer.

Langdon remembered seeing the cross at Laneast churchyard as late as 1886 but upon re-visiting the site in 1890 he was surprised to find the stone removed. Later, when visiting Tresmeer, he found the cross had been re-erected as a memorial stone on the eastern side of the churchyard on the grave of Rev. Morgan.

The Latin cross displays a similar cross in relief on each face and closely resembles the head of the cross at St. Cleer Holy Well.

Height (above ground) 1' 8" (0.51M), Width of head 1' 9" (0.535M), Width of shaft 8 1/2" (0.215M), Thickness 6" (0.15M).

100

Cross Fragment in Church Porch Tresmeer

FOUR HOLED CHURCHYARD CROSS

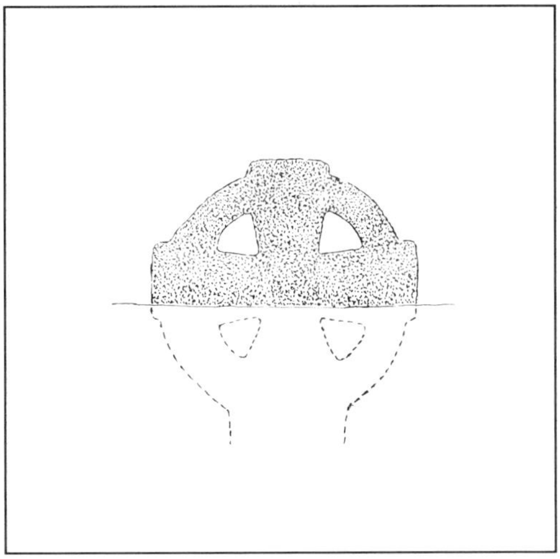

SX 2335, 8747 - Built into the eastern wall inside the south porch of the parish church. Access - Unlimited.

This fragment of a four holed cross - the upper half of the cross head - was, according to Ellis, discovered in 1878 by the vicar, the Rev. R.P. Roberts. It was later built into the porch wall in 1880 for preservation when the church was re-built.

The fragment is very worn, and all signs of decoration have been erased, the holes formed by the cross limbs and outer ring are almost triangular due to the limbs being expanded at their extremities.

Width of head 2' 2" (0.66M), Height of remaining fragment 1' 4 1/2" (0.42M), Thickness 9" (0.23M).

101

Youlstone No. 1 Warbstow

WHEEL HEADED BOUNDARY OR WAYSIDE CROSS

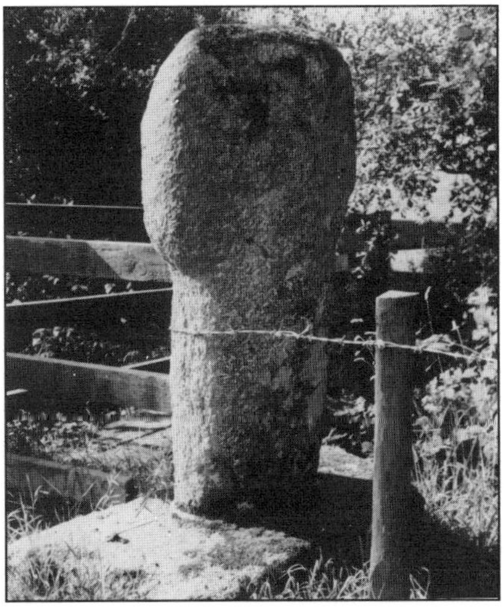

SX 1982, 8949 - On a footpath between the farms of Trewonnard and Youlstone, close to a footbridge across a stream. Access - Unlimited, the cross stands beside a public footpath..

A footpath which in the past was the old church path, runs north-east from Trewonnard Farm down across a steep field to a tributary of the river Attery. A footbridge straddles the small stream and beside it stands the Youlstone Cross. The footpath continues up through Youlstone Farm towards the churchtown.

Langdon recorded the cross in 1896 under Lower Youlston. In his day the monument was in use as a bridge across the stream. He stated that the upper face of the stone had been worn away due to people walking across it. The stream divides the parishes of Treneglos and Warbstow and the cross may have served a dual purpose as a church path guide and parish bound stone. Ellis had great difficulty in finding the monument in 1938 and after an extensive search it was discovered built into the river bank supporting wooden sleepers which formed the bridge. It was due to Ellis that the monument was re-erected, financial support coming from St. Ives Old Cornwall Society.

Height 3' 10" (1.17M), Width of head 2' (0.61M), Width of shaft (at neck) 1' 6" (0.46M), Width of shaft (at base) 1' 4" (0.41M), Thickness 8" (0.2M).

Youlstone No. 2
Warbstow
WHEEL HEADED WAYSIDE CROSS

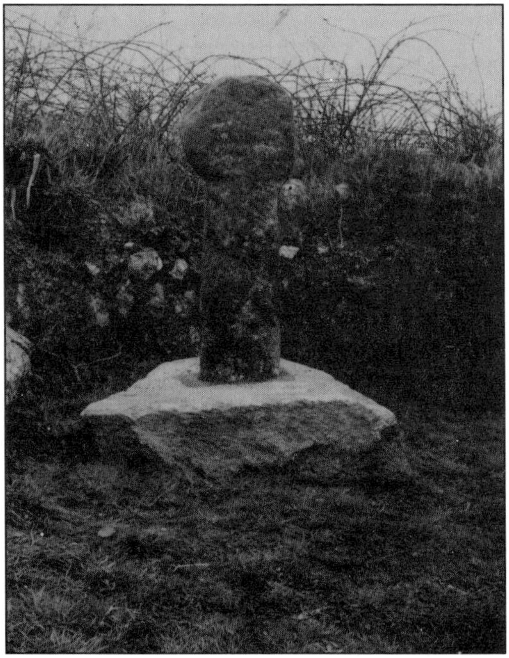

SX 1986, 8957 - At Youlstone Farm, one mile south-west of Warbstow parish church. Access - The cross stands beside the farm drive which is a public footpath, the surrounding land is private.

In 1973 a second cross was discovered at Youlstone Farm in use as a gatepost, buried head down in the ground. This cross displayed an incised Latin cross on either side of a round head. It, too, probably marked part of the old church path and was found on ground at Higher Youlstone. In March 1996 permission was gained from the landowner to re-erect the monument and a project was organised by Mr. David Attwell from the North Cornwall Heritage Coast and Countryside Service. A new base stone was cut from a piece of moorland granite with the help of stonemasons Mr. Noel Hill and Mr. E. Hillson.

On Thursday 14th. March the base stone was transported to the farm, and placed beside the farm drive close to the farmhouse. The cross was then lifted into position by the landowner Mr. M. Shute with the assistance of both Mr. Attwell and the author. The mortice in the base stone was cut large enough to receive a small portion of the shaft which was then set in place with a lime putty cement.

Height 5' (1.52M), Width of head 1' 5 1/2" (0.44M), Width of shaft (at neck) 10 1/2" (0.27M), Width of shaft (at base) 12 1/2" (0.32M), Thickness 8" (0.2M).

List of Stones not featured in this Guide

The following list gives a brief reference to the many fragments of crosses not featured in this guide. The majority are cross bases, although some are stones of doubtful origin and are difficult to authenticate, they are therefore recorded as "possibles".

Row, St. Breward SX 0956, 7654 CROSS BASE
Unlimited public access. The stone is built into the foot of the hedge, near a cottage called "Wayside", between Limehead and St. Breward Post Office.

Churchtown, St. Breward SX 0975, 7722 CROSS BASE
Unlimited public access. The stone stands between the old village shute (spring) at the entrance to the village hall, on the right-hand side of the road leading from Row to the parish church.

Churchyard, Davidstow SX 1511, 8726 GOTHIC GABLE CROSS
Unlimited public access. The stone stands on the grave of Charlotte Dymond, murdered in 1844 at Roughtor. The cross probably fell off the church at some stage and was later placed as a memorial stone on the south side of the churchyard.

Churchyard, St. Ervan SW 8919, 7026 POSSIBLE CROSS BASE
Unlimited public access. The stone lies just outside of the churchyard on the right-hand side of the lych gate. It has an unusual right angled mortice, which suggests an element of doubt to its original purpose.

Lancarffe, Helland SX 0818, 6895 GOTHIC CROSS BASE
The stone is on private ground, there is no public access unless the grounds are open to the public, usually about twice a year. The base is the former pedestal, which the lantern cross (No. 40 in this guide) once stood on.

Lower Kernick, Helland SX 0848, 7130 CROSS BASE
The cross base leans against a barn on private ground, although it can be seen clearly from the public road. It was removed from the parish of Lewannick about twenty years ago.

Downhead, Laneast SX 2322, 8471 CROSS BASE
The cross base lies surrounded in thick gorse and bracken on a small triangular piece of waste ground, near the junction between the A395 Davidstow to Launceston road and a minor road to Laneast. The author was unable to establish whether the land is privately owned.

Lawrence House Museum, St. Mary Magdalene SX 3306, 8472 CROSS HEAD/QUERN
Public access is available - please check opening times and admission charges. The stone has an equal limbed cross cut on one face, but has been possibly re-used as a quern.

Churchyard, St. Stephens by Launceston SX 3247, 8569 GABLE CROSS
Unlimited public access. A small gable cross stands on a grave of the Ching Langdon family, close to the south-west angle of the church. The cross was probably attached to the church at one time.

Churchyard, St. Thomas by Launceston SX 3280, 8507 OCTAGONAL PEDESTAL
Unlimited public access. Opposite the south porch of the church is an octagonal plinth, made up of layers of slate, and may have once supported a cross or even a sundial.

Near Tredethy, St. Mabyn SX 0578, 7210 POSSIBLE GOTHIC CROSS SHAFT
Unlimited public access. This octagonal granite shaft today supports a 19th century granite direction post but has all the appearance of the shaft of a Gothic Latin cross. It stands near a staggered crossroads, the fields either side of which are known as Great and Little Cross Mould.

Church Porch, St. Mabyn SX 0419, 7318 GOTHIC GABLE CROSS
There is public access when the church is unlocked. The fragments of this gable cross lie in the church porch and appear to have recently fallen off the church.

Trenant Steading, St. Minver SW 9440, 7929 POSSIBLE CROSS BASE
There is no public access, the stone is on private grounds. It consists of a massive granite stone with a mortice cut straight through it. The stone is fractured and was originally discovered at Roserrow Farm, St. Minver.

Bush Inn, Morwenstow SS 2073, 1507 CROSS HEAD OR CHEESE PRESS
There is no public access to view the stone. It is built into an inner wall in the private part of the Inn, and its authenticity is in doubt. It has been suggested that it is either a base of a cheese press or a coffin slab.

Churchyard, Morwenstow SS 2055, 1530 HAWKER MEMORIAL CROSS
Unlimited public access. This cross stands on the grave of the wife of Parson Hawker and although recorded in guide books as being ancient, in the author's opinion is far from ancient and gives the impression of being a modern 19th. century copy.

St. John's Well, Morwenstow SS 2051,1540 SEMI-GOTHIC CROSS ON HOLY WELL
On the holy well of St. John the Baptist in the old vicarage garden at Morwenstow is a small Latin cross of octagonal section mounted on the gable of the building. The author is not sure whether this cross was originally a gable or free standing cross. The well is situated on private ground, although there is a permissive path from the end of the churchyard.

Churchyard, North Tamerton SX 3119, 9732 GOTHIC CROSS BASE
Unlimited public access, this cross base lies on the south side of the churchyard, on the right hand side of the south porch.

Churchyard, Otterham SX 1683, 9073 CROSS SLAB/COFFIN SLAB
Unlimited public access. This small slate slab leans against the south porch of the parish church, and displays a rough Latin cross in relief, if the stone is a coffin slab it must be for a child as the stone is only 2ft 9ins (0.84M) in length.

In Parish Church, Padstow SW 9156, 7541 GABLE CROSS/WINDOW MULLION
Public access, normally during daylight hours. The stone in the form of a Gothic Latin cross stands just inside the door from the north porch, it has the appearance of being cut from an old window mullion.

Prideaux Place, Padstow SW 9130, 7553 FRAGMENT OF CROSS SHAFT
Public access to the grounds is limited, check opening times and admission charges, there is no free admission. The fragment of shaft was retrieved from under the roots of a tree on the estate in 1988 and is now beside the four holed cross on the lawn.

The Stables, St. Teath SX 0648, 8056 POSSIBLE CROSS HEAD

The stone stands in private grounds, there is no public access to it. It displays faint traces of a cross but must be considered as of doubtful antiquity.

Castle Site, Tintagel SX 0517, 8890 STONES DISPLAYING CROSSES

There is no public access, the stones are at present locked away. They were both discovered in recent archaeological work at Tintagel Castle in 1988 and display equal limbed crosses in relief.

Tintagel Churchyard, Tintagel INCISED CROSSES ON SLATE

During excavations by the County Archaeological Unit in 1990 and 1991, fragments of slate were found in use as covers to Cist graves in the churchyard displaying incised crosses with expanded limbs.

Rectory Grounds, Tintagel SX 0549,8841 GABLE CROSS

There is no public access, the small greenstone gable cross stands on private ground. It was first recorded by Blight in 1858, but has now lost one of its horizontal limbs. It measures 18 ins. (0.46M) in height and stands 3 metres west of the medieval culverhouse in the grounds.

Hengar Manor, St. Tudy SX 0797, 7700 GABLE CROSS

There is no public access. The stone is on private grounds and is situated on the gable of a barn on the estate, which is now a holiday park.

Stones Recorded but now Missing

Callywith, Bodmin	Half a cross base, discovered during by-pass construction.
Bore Street, Bodmin	Cross base in use as a doorstop and shaft buried in wall of house.
St. Nicholas House, Bodmin	Possible cross head in the grounds.
Churchtown Bridge, St. Breward	Further fragments of the churchyard cross.
Gamm Bridge, St. Breward	Cross base beside the bridge.
Moor Lane, St. Breward	Cross base by the roadside.
Cargelly, St. Breward	Cross base.
West Rose Farm, St. Breward	Cross base.
Trescowe Farm, Egloshayle	Cross shaft on the farm.
Rooke Mill, St. Kew	Fragments of a four holed cross lying in a stream.
Parish Church, Laneast	Fragment of a four holed cross head, once preserved in the church
Old Vicarage garden wall, Padstow	Two gable crosses
Churchyard, St. Teath	Cross base in churchyard.

Chronology of Recent Cross Discoveries in Cornwall

March 1984*	St. Just in Penwith	LATIN CROSS	SW 3524,3185
August 1984	Trevilley, Sennen	CROSS BASE	SW 3570,2464
April 1984*	Hendra, Menheniot	WHEEL HEADED CROSS	SX 2697,6545
December 1986*	Tredinick, St. Breock	CROSS HEAD	SW 9722,7212
August 1987	Trelights, St. Endellion	CROSS BASE	SW 9902,7876
April 1988*	Penrose, Wendron	FRAGMENT OF CROSS HEAD	SW 6413,2576
1988*	Castle Site, Tintagel	TWO CARVED STONES DISPLAYING CROSSES	
October 1988	Tregonning, Luxulyan	CROSS HEAD	SX 0539,5702
December 1988*	Tregurtha, St. Wenn	CROSS HEAD	SW 9586,6447
April 1989*	Trevadlock, Lewannick	GOTHIC CROSS HEAD	SX 2651,7902
February 1989	Rostigan, St. Wenn	CROSS SHAFT	SW 9718,6468
May 1989	Tregrylls, Lesnewth	LATIN CROSS	SX 1269,8944
January 1990	Lower Kernick, Helland	CROSS BASE	SX 0848,7130
September 1990	Menawink, Lanlivery	WHEEL HEADED CROSS	SX 0711,5958
July 1991	Lamorrick, Lanivet	WHEEL HEADED CROSS	SX 0358,6460
June 1993	High Cross, Constantine	WHEEL HEADED CROSS	Site to be arranged.
June 1994*	Trefranck, St.Clether	WHEEL HEADED CROSS	" "

* The asterisk indicates crosses that are on private ground with no public access at present, other monuments recorded here may be on private ground but are beside public footpaths or rights of way.

Glossary

ABACUS	A collar-like disc around the neck of a stone cross.
BEAD	A narrow moulding of semi-circular section, seen around the head and down the sides of many Cornish crosses.
BENCHMARK	Broad arrow symbol carved on stone by surveyors to mark reference point of levels, usually cut by Ordnance Survey.
BOSS	Carved or sculptured projection, which is normally half round.
CHAMFERED	A bevelled edge running down the shaft of a monument.
CROSS - CROSSLET	An equal limbed cross, with additional crosses formed on each limb.
CUSPS	Projecting point between two arcs in Gothic tracery or in the holes of a four holed cross.
DISC HEADED	This is another name for a round or wheel head of a cross.
ENTASIS	Slight convexity of a column or shaft provided to correct the visual illusion of concavity.
EXPANDED LIMBS	Limbs that are not of a uniform width, but wider at the ends than at the centre.
GLEBE	Land attached to the parish church.
INCISED CROSS	Cross cut into a piece of material, rather than being carved in a raised position.
INTERLACE WORK	Celtic style decoration consisting of cords in a plaited form.
MINUSCULES	7th century script in small letters instead of capitals (Anglo Saxon).
MONOLITH	Single large block or pillar of stone.
MORTICE	Hole or socket cut into a base stone to receive the tenon of a cross.
OGHAM (OGAM)	British/Irish alphabet consisting of straight lines across or either side of a continuous line.
PEDESTAL	Raised base stone or support for a cross.

PLINTH	Similar to a pedestal, a support or base stone for a monument.
PROJECTIONS	Protrusions at the neck of a wheel headed cross.
REBATED	In a few cases, instead of having a bead around the head and shaft of a cross, a similar effect is produced by reducing the thickness on the edge of the monument.
RELIEF	A cross cut in relief, is a method of carving where the design stands out from the surface in a raised position.
RELIQUARY	A receptacle for the placing of relics.
RING	The segment of stone joining adjacent limbs of a four holed cross.
TENON	Projecting section of stone at the bottom of a cross shaft to fit into a corresponding socket (mortice) in a base stone.
TREFOIL HOLES	Holes in the shape of a three part leaf.
TREQUETRA KNOTS	Symmetrical decoration formed from three interlaced arcs.
TRIANGULAR SINKINGS	Four triangular depressions arranged in a pattern to form a cross shape.

Parts of a Stone Cross

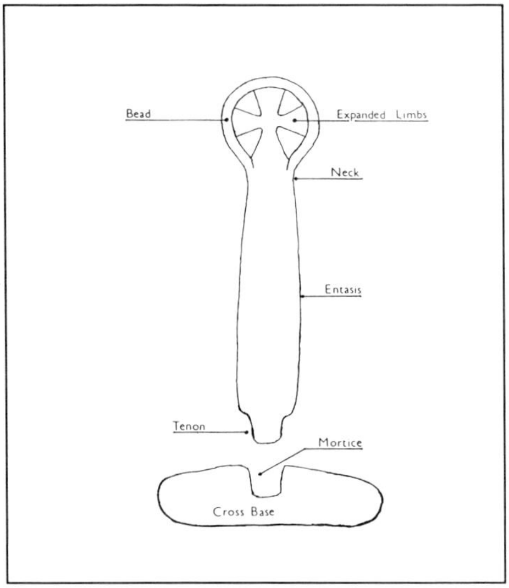

Wheel Headed Cross

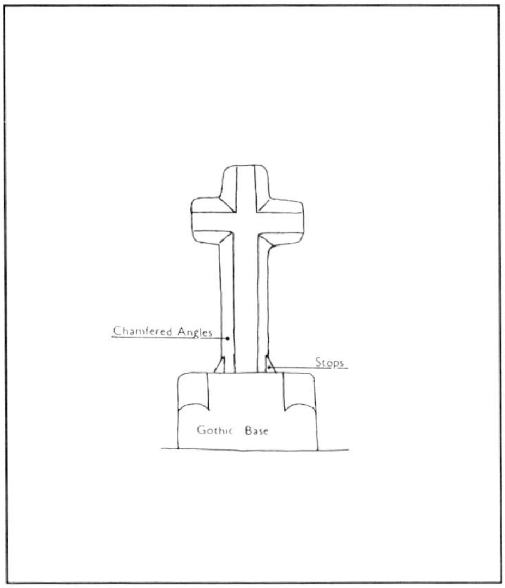

Gothic Latin Cross

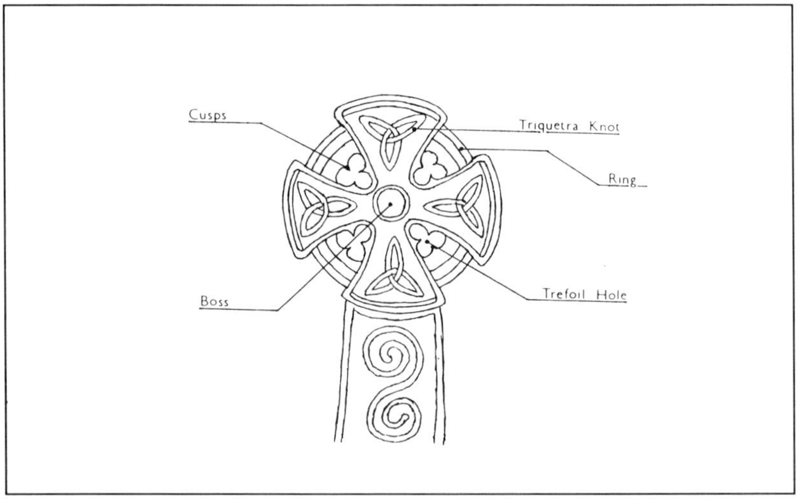

Celtic Style Cross

Bibliography

For the serious student there are many papers and major works on the study of Cornish crosses, most of which are available at local libraries, although a few unpublished works are housed in the Royal Institution of Cornwall's Courtney Library at Truro.

BORLASE, W. — Antiquities Historical and Monumental of the County of Cornwall 1754.

HINGSTON RANDOLPH, F.C. — Specimens of Ancient Cornish crosses and Fonts 1850.

BLIGHT, J.T. — Ancient Crosses and Antiquities in West Cornwall 1856.

BLIGHT, J.T. — Ancient Crosses and Antiquities in East Cornwall 1858.

BLIGHT, J.T. — A second edition in 1872, combined both West and East Cornwall's crosses under one cover.

MACLEAN, SIR J. — The Parochial and Family History of the Deanery of Trigg Minor (3 Vols. dated 1873, 1876 and 1879).

IAGO, REV. W. — Personal sketch book on Stone Crosses and Ecclesiastic monuments 1876.

IAGO, REV. W. — Many papers on Crosses and inscribed stones in various Royal Institution of Cornwall journals.

LANGDON A:G. and ROMILLY ALLEN J. — The Early Christian Monuments of Cornwall paper published by the British Archaeological Association 1888.

LANGDON, A.G. — The Ornament on the Early Crosses of Cornwall Journal paper published in the Royal Institution of Cornwall Journal Vol. X part 1 May 1890 (pp. 33 - 96).

LANGDON , A.G. — Old Cornish Crosses 1896 (reprinted in 1988 by Cornwall Books).

LANGDON, A.G. — The Victoria County History of Cornwall 1906, Vol. 1 (chapter on the Early Christian Monuments).

LANGDON, A.G. — Collection of additional drawings dated between 1894 and 1909 housed in the Courtney Library, R.I.C. Truro.

STEPHENS, W.J. — St. Kew Crosses, paper published in the Royal Institution of Cornwall Journal Vol. XX 1915)p. 89).

HENDERSON, C.G. — Notes for a Supplement to A.G. Langdon's Old Cornish Crosses 1930, housed in the Courtney Library, R.I.C. Truro.

HENDERSON, C.G.	Missing Cornish Crosses, a paper published in the Old Cornwall Society Journal Vol. 1 No. 12 Winter 1930 (p.6).
HENDERSON, C.G.	Essays in Cornish History 1933, chapter entitled Cornish crosses after Langdon's day. (pp. 193 - 196).
DEXTER, T.F.G. & H.	Cornish Crosses, Christian and Pagan 1938.
ELLIS, G.E.	Cornish Crosses, published in the Devon & Cornwall Notes & Queries Journal, between 1952 and 1968.
BAIRD, MAJOR R.D. & LADY WHITE	Cornish Crosses 1961, typed manuscript housed in the Courtney Library, R.I.C. Truro.
ROWE, L.	Granite Crosses of West Cornwall 1973.
HENDERSON, M.	A Survey of Ancient Crosses of Cornwall 1952 - 1983. A four volume 1091 page manuscript, accompanied with one volume of illustrations by L. Rowe.
LANGDON, Andrew G.	Stone Crosses in North Cornwall 1992 (1st. Edition).
LANGDON, Andrew G.	Stone Crosses in Mid Cornwall 1994.
LANGDON, Andrew G.	Stone Crosses in East Cornwall 1996.
LANGDON Andrew G.	Note on Cornish Crosses in various Old Cornwall Society Journals, Vol. X and XI, 1986 onwards.

Archaeology

BORLASE W.	Antiquities Historical and Monumental of the County of Cornwall 1754.
MACALISTER R.A.S.	Archaeological Cambrensis 1929 Vol. 84.
HENCKEN H. O'Neill	Archaeology of Cornwall & Isles of Scilly 1932.
WOOLF C.	An Introduction to the Archaeology of Cornwall 1970.
PEARCE S.	The Kingdom of Dumnonia 1978.
WEATHERHILL C.	Cornovia - Ancient Sites of Cornwall & Scilly 1985.
THOMAS A.C.	Celtic Britain 1986.

There are many more references to Cornish crosses contained in Cornish history books, journals and in manuscript form. The above list represents some of the most important works only and not a complete list.